The Art of Extreme Self-Care

Also by Cheryl Richardson

Books

Take Time for Your Life: *A Personal Coach's Seven-Step Program for Creating the Life You Want*

Life Makeovers: *52 Practical and Inspiring Ways to Improve Your Life One Week at a Time*

Stand Up for Your Life: *Develop the Courage, Confidence, and Character to Fulfill Your Greatest Potential*

The Unmistakable Touch of Grace: *How to Recognize and Respond to the Spiritual Signposts in Your Life*

Turning Inward: *A Private Journal of Self-Reflection**

Audio Programs

Finding Your Passion (4-CD program)*

Tuning In: *Listening to the Voice of Your Soul* (CD)*

Experience the Power of Grace (6-CD program)*

Card Decks

Grace Cards (a 50-card deck)*

Self-Care Cards (a 52-card deck)*

*Available from Hay House

Please visit Hay House USA: www.hayhouse.com®
Hay House Australia: **www.hayhouse.com.au**
Hay House UK: **www.hayhouse.co.uk**
Hay House South Africa: **www.hayhouse.co.za**
Hay House India: **www.hayhouse.co.in**

The Art of Extreme Self-Care

Transform Your Life One Month at a Time

Cheryl Richardson

HAY HOUSE, INC.
Carlsbad, California • New York City
London • Sydney • Johannesburg
Vancouver • Hong Kong • New Delhi

Published and distributed in the United States by: Hay House, Inc.: www.hayhouse.com • *Published and distributed in Australia by:* Hay House Australia Pty. Ltd.: www.hayhouse.com.au • *Published and distributed in the United Kingdom by:* Hay House UK, Ltd.: www.hayhouse.co.uk • *Published and distributed in the Republic of South Africa by:* Hay House SA (Pty), Ltd.: www.hayhouse.co.za • *Distributed in Canada by:* Raincoast: www.raincoast.com • *Published in India by:* Hay House Publishers India: www.hayhouse.co.in

Editorial supervision: Jill Kramer   •   *Design:* Amy Rose Grigoriou

The author gratefully acknowledges Thomas Leonard, founder of Coach University and **www. coachville.com**, and one of the earliest formulators of the concept of Extreme Self-Care.

Library of Congress Control Number: 2006940287

ISBN: 978-1-4019-1828-6

12 11 10 09   4 3 2 1
1st edition, January 2009

Printed in the United States of America

To Michael, my one and only love . . .

Contents

Introduction

In 1994, I made a decision to hire my first personal coach. Although I thought this decision would make me a better coach myself, it turned out to do much more. It gave me a better life. Thomas Leonard, founder of Coach University and the leading pioneer in the field of professional coaching, was the man's name, and I'll never forget what happened in our first session.

During the intake process, Thomas asked me to tell him a little about my life. He wanted to get a sense of who I was and how I lived. For the next 20 minutes, I talked about all the things that occupied my time:

- I worked as a business-development counselor at night and on weekends.
- I taught career-planning seminars for a corporate consulting firm.
- I volunteered for a local job-search organization, offering workshops on interviewing and networking skills.
- I supported friends who were struggling and needed a selfless, compassionate ear.

As I listened to myself talk about my schedule, I have to admit that I felt pretty good. There was a certain level of satisfaction that came from being needed and in demand. When I finished, Thomas was quiet for a moment, and then, with a slight edge in his voice, said, "Wow, you do a great job of taking care of a lot of people. You're such a good person."

I smiled to myself, thinking, *Hmm, he really gets me.* But what he said next took me totally by surprise: "And the truth is, Cheryl, your 'good girl' role is going to rob you of your life."

I sat still for what felt like a very long time. My moment of triumph slowly turned to tears as Thomas's words hit home. I *was* a good girl. I was so used to playing the role of caretaker that it had become a normal way of life. It had also become my identity and how I defined my self-worth. Now, many years and many clients later, I know I wasn't alone. So many of us, especially women, have taken on this "noble" role. What we don't realize—until it's too late—is the high price we pay for being "so generous" . . . a price extracted from our very bones.

While at that time I thought I felt good about caring for others, when it came time to talk with Thomas about what wasn't working in my life, my complaints revealed something quite different. I had to admit that I had no time for myself. I felt resentful about helping to make others successful yet never getting around to doing what I wanted to do. I also had to face the reality that too many of my relationships were one-way streets. Some of my friends were extremely needy, yet I kept them in my life because they made me feel safe, in control, and significant. Yes, Thomas was right: I was a good girl, and it was sucking the life out of me.

It was during our work together that Thomas introduced me to the concept of Extreme Self-Care. The word *extreme* intrigued me and got my attention. I remember feeling excited about the idea, but also a little nervous. From Thomas's perspective, Extreme Self-Care meant taking my care to a whole new level—a level that, to me, seemed arrogant and selfish, practiced by people who had an inappropriate sense of entitlement. It meant taking radical action to improve my life *and* engaging in daily habits that allowed me to maintain this new standard of living. For example, it wasn't enough to take a weekend off from helping others so that I could enjoy some downtime. Thomas wanted me to schedule time for myself (on my calendar, in ink) *every day* for six months.

Extreme Self-Care also involved surrounding myself with people who were smart, self-aware, and only interested in two-way relationships. It meant taking bold steps, such as eliminating clutter from my life, for good; creating a soul-nourishing work and home environment, and keeping it that way; getting my financial act together so that I always had choices about how to live my life; and not making any commitments whatsoever out of guilt or obligation.

In addition, Thomas explained that making pleasure a priority was critical for Extreme Self-Care—real pleasure, not just a massage every couple of months, an occasional bath, or a yearly vacation. It meant leaving work in the middle of the day to get out into nature, enjoying a great massage once a week, and developing daily habits that made me feel happy and nurtured, including listening to the music I loved, drinking

my favorite tea, or ordering fresh flowers for my office.

At first I had great resistance to the idea of Extreme Self-Care. A massage once a week? How could I ever afford that when I had to pay my rent? Time to myself every day? I could barely find time to go to the bathroom, let alone for a walk at lunch. My coach's suggestions seemed idealistic, bordering on absurd. But, as I would soon discover, *a great life starts with an open mind.* To this day, I'm thankful that Thomas Leonard had a higher vision for my life than I had for myself.

As I slowly began to incorporate Extreme Self-Care into my life, it was clear that internal changes were required in order to make these behaviors stick. For example, I needed to quit being a martyr and focus on getting my needs met. I had to stop expecting others to read my mind and start being direct about what I wanted. I was challenged to try asking for help long before I needed it. Rather than bitch and moan about how others had let me down, I was to see my frustration as an indication that something needed to change. I also had to begin asking people to share the load instead of being a hero by attempting to do it all myself. Finally, I had to stop being an automatic yes machine when people asked for my help and instead learn to say no with confidence and ease.

As the work Thomas and I did together progressed, I discovered that making these changes wasn't easy. When I look back now, I can see that I was challenging a legacy of self-sacrifice and overgiving passed down to me by generations of women in my family—the same legacy that confounds so many women even now. Too many of us are continuing to be the good girl, and it's a tough habit to break. I still catch myself doing this when I feel stressed and under pressure. Suddenly I'm bending over backward to make it easier for an employee to do his or her job (I call this "hiring people to work for"). Or I'm scheduling too many activities into a day to accommodate the needs of everyone else (I call this "insanity"). For those of us who do such things—and this includes men as well as women—it's often an automatic response, as if a default button gets pushed and we reflexively revert to these behaviors.

The Rewards of Extreme Self-Care

A good coach focuses on the source of a problem rather than the symptoms. In my work with Thomas, I was forced to look at the truth of why I continued to give too much, usually at my own expense. I wanted people to like me, to enjoy spending time with me, and to see me as wise and helpful. I also wanted to avoid the anxiety I felt whenever someone disapproved of something I did. Funny, but after years of practicing Extreme Self-Care, I've realized something ironic: if you want to live an authentic,

meaningful life, you need to master the art of disappointing and upsetting others, hurting feelings, and living with the reality that some people just won't like you. It may not be easy, but it's essential if you want your life to reflect your deepest desires, values, and needs.

Over time, as my life became more oriented around the principles of Extreme Self-Care, it began to have a positive impact on my work. As a coach, I passed on what Thomas had taught me by challenging my clients to accept no less than the highest possible standards—be it for their work, their relationships, their health, or just their overall well-being. When they did, their lives changed dramatically—it was as if they became more aligned with a divine energy or force that opened doors to support their highest good. But even though the idea was intriguing and fun to consider, it wasn't always easy getting people on board. As much as Americans are portrayed as an overindulgent society, the truth is that when we decide to care for ourselves in a more attentive, proactive, and soul-nourishing way, we're forced to confront a cultural view that *selfish* is a dirty word.

The concept of making one's self-care a priority remains controversial to this very day. Over the years I've repeatedly had to defend this idea to the media as well as to clients and audience members. Now I welcome the opportunity, and here's why: the practice of Extreme Self-Care forces us to make choices and decisions that honor and reflect the true nature of our soul. While the whole notion of this might seem selfish or self-centered, doing so actually allows us to make our greatest contribution to the world. The choice to live a life that reflects the tenets of Extreme Self-Care is critical if we want to make a difference in the world . . . and most people I know do.

From years of personal experience, as well as from the work I've done coaching many caring and hardworking men and women, I've learned that when we care for ourselves deeply and deliberately, we naturally begin to care for others—our families, our friends, and the world—in a healthier and more effective way. We become conscious *and* conscientious people. We tell the truth. We make choices from a place of love and compassion instead of guilt and obligation. And we begin to understand—on a visceral level—that we're all connected, and that our individual actions affect the greater whole in a more profound way than we ever imagined. A CEO who never gave much thought to recycling, for instance, finds that his own awakening to Extreme Self-Care leads him to not only take better care of himself and his family, but to also start a recycling plan at work. Or a mom who learns to make her own needs a priority (rather than always attending to her children first) develops a program to help mothers raise more confident and independent kids.

Enjoying a life of Extreme Self-Care means living and working in a soul-nurturing environment; developing a greater appreciation for, and connection with, nature; doing work that provides an opportunity to express your greatest gifts and talents; and caring for your emotional, physical, and spiritual health in a way that's aligned with who you are and what you most need. When you allow yourself to want this and then have it, you can't help but want it for others as well.

The art of Extreme Self-Care takes patience, commitment, and practice. It initially requires a willingness to sit with some pretty uncomfortable feelings, too, such as guilt—for putting your own needs first, fear—of being judged and criticized by others, or anxiety—from challenging long-held beliefs and behaviors. It's an organic, evolutionary process; an art as opposed to a science. Over time, you'll make progress and become more comfortable with the process, but you'll also regress. I know the dance well. There are days when I set firm limits on my availability so that I don't feel overwhelmed with work, yet there are other days when I'm beating myself up, wondering why the hell I'm still in the office at 9 P.M. The difference today is that I'm much more aware of what it feels like when I'm getting into trouble, and I know what I have to do to get back on course.

During the past 15 years, the rich and fruitful life I've experienced has been a direct result of practicing Extreme Self-Care. Because I know that there are no quick fixes—and we're talking about challenging a way of life, not rearranging a room—I've designed this book to help *you* practice it by taking small steps every month. Each of the following 12 chapters offers you a different way to do so, and at the end of every one, you'll find an "Extreme Self-Care Challenge" with guidelines and suggestions for getting and staying on track. You'll also find some of my favorite resources, which will offer you additional ways to pursue and sustain your individual self-care goals.

(**Editors note:** All italized titles in the resource sections refer to books, unless othewise noted.)

Set Yourself Up to Succeed

If you like being held accountable when attempting to make changes, set yourself up to succeed by enlisting a good friend or, better yet, *a group* of like-minded people to accompany you on your journey. If you don't have someone in mind, or you feel uncomfortable with the idea of assembling a group, don't worry. Just visit **www.cherylrichardson.com** and check out the Life Makeover Group section. This wonderful online community, which includes thousands of people from all over the world who have been supporting one another for many years, provides free resources to help you make connections in your area. When you join a Life Makeover Group, you'll soon find yourself practicing Extreme Self-Care with a wide variety of caring and helpful people who are committed to changing their lives. By following the guidelines on this site, you'll also learn how to form and run a successful group of your own.

As you get started on this life-changing journey, be mindful of what types of changes would benefit you most at this time in your life. To develop a clearer perspective of this, I suggest that you read the entire book first. When you finish, if you're not sure which chapter to begin with, pick the one you'd most like to avoid, and then get to work. Make Extreme Self-Care a consistent part of your daily life. And remember, not only will it be the greatest gift you give to yourself, it will be the greatest gift you give to others, too.

Okay, are you ready to transform your life? Dramatically, and for good? Then let's get started! Good luck, and I hope you enjoy the ride. . . .

Resources

❈ Coach University (**www.coachu.com**)—for information on finding a coach and becoming one yourself, including coach training.

❈ CoachVille (**www.coachville.com**)—a Website dedicated to coaches that provides content, community, and a curriculum for coaches from all walks of life. There is lots of great information from Thomas Leonard, written before he passed away in 2003.

❈ The International Coach Federation (**www.coachfederation.org**)—the largest independent professional association for coaches worldwide, it also offers a coach-referral service.

❈ My own Website (**www.cherylrichardson.com**)—for information on finding or starting a Life Makeover Group in your area, along with resources on how to run a successful group meeting.

❈ My weekly Internet radio show, "Coach on Call" (at **HayHouseRadio.com**®)—if you'd like to receive live coaching from me directly.

Chapter One

End the Legacy of Deprivation

Every book I write presents me with a challenging and unexpected opportunity to practice what I teach. By now I've learned that I should always count on something happening that will force me to engage in an intensive study on the subject of each chapter. What you're now reading is no exception.

Once I signed on to write about Extreme Self-Care, my husband got very sick. During surgery to have a small lump removed from his ear, he had a complication that affected his health in a serious way for more than two years. The timing was particularly bad. Not only was I running a company, hosting a weekly radio show, traveling to speaking engagements, and writing a book, but we were also in the final stages of building our dream home—a stressful undertaking that had been Michael's focus for the better part of three years.

As Michael found himself less able to monitor, and put energy into, the project (he was making critical decisions regarding the design of the house), I was faced with taking over some of his responsibilities in between doctor and pharmacy visits, as well as giving him the emotional support he needed to survive this very difficult time.

When hit with an unexpected life challenge, most of us revert back to the old coping strategies that kept us safe as kids. For example, you may have taken refuge in your bedroom to avoid dealing with parents who always fought. As an adult, when faced with a chaotic situation such as losing a job or dealing with challenges in your own marriage, you now find yourself isolating from others as a way to escape the stress. You don't ask for help. You don't reach out for emotional support. And you don't admit to yourself or others the way you really feel. Instead, you suffer in silence.

In spite of what I know about self-care, I'm no different. Several weeks following Michael's surgery, I found myself in "rescue mode" as I tried to juggle his needs with the demands of building our new home, managing my business, and writing this book. I made long to-do lists in an effort to keep myself on track. I flitted from one thing to another in a state of perpetual multitasking and often woke up in the middle of the night feeling anxious, ruminating about all that needed to get done. As my stress level increased, I started using food to stuff my feelings of resentment and frustration—a common response for caregivers who are always on call for someone in need. I felt like a pressure cooker ready to blow and, as a result, I did what I normally do when faced with having too much to do: I sucked it up, hunkered down, ignored my needs, and tried to do everything myself. Most days I felt alone and afraid, but I never told anyone. I just kept forging ahead. It wasn't long before I found myself struggling to stay afloat, barely able to tread water. What had happened to Extreme Self-Care?

I lived with the irony of my situation day in and day out. Here I was writing about Extreme Self-Care, but my life was reading like an advertisement for the exact opposite—extreme disrepair! To say I was running on fumes would be an understatement. My tank wasn't empty; it was MIA.

Eventually, when I was forced to admit that I was in over my head, I sought guidance from a professional who had experience supporting caregivers in crisis. She turned out to be a godsend—the right person at the right time. One day during a session, she touched a nerve with an observation. After listening to me complain about how exhausted I was, she said, "It seems to me that when you feel burdened, Cheryl, you do the opposite of what a human being needs to do. Instead of clearing the decks, asking for help, and giving yourself space to breathe, you fall into a pattern of self-neglect. Rather than asking *yourself* what you need, you shift into overdrive and immerse yourself in the needs of others. I'd say it's time to put an end to this legacy of deprivation, wouldn't you?"

Deprivation. Hmm. Now there was a concept I hadn't considered. *Deprivation. Deprived. Deprive.* I sat there for a while, letting variations of the word roll around in my head. *Yup, that's it,* I ultimately decided. *I feel deprived.* Although I was considered an expert in self-care, when faced with a crisis I had reverted back to my old coping habits. I'd fly solo, often encountering turbulence, but always steering toward familiar territory: a place where I automatically focused on others' needs, avoided talking about myself, and was the first to lend a hand when someone else needed a lift. But now I was tired—exhausted, really—and fed up with being a martyr. It was time to do something about it.

When I went home that day, I sat on my bed, pulled out my journal, and wrote the following in it:

I feel deprived of:

- *Sleep*

- *Emotional support*

- *Time to myself*

- *Physical energy*

- *Companionship—I miss Michael, my partner and my best friend*

- *Peace—I worry all the time*

- *Hope—I'm afraid things won't get any better*

- *Touch—I miss the affection and closeness I normally have with Michael*

As I looked at this list, I thought, *No wonder I feel so empty and resentful all the time. I'm back to being the good girl who takes on too much and complains about it afterward.* Yes, I was dealing with extenuating circumstances in caring for a sick loved one, but all the more reason to practice good self-care, right?

Fortunately, I had enough experience under my belt to know what to do. *Awareness is a powerful catalyst for positive change,* and as I started to recognize how deprived I felt, I immediately began to put Extreme Self-Care into practice. I started by clearing my plate. I let go of almost 50 percent of what I was working on to give me the emotional and physical space to be there for Michael and myself. I delayed the deadline for my book, put limits on phone calls and e-mails, and stopped scheduling all of my time. The goal was to give myself more breathing room than I thought I needed. I put some business projects on hold and eliminated those that caused me any stress. I also lined up some friends to be on call when I needed to vent, and I started asking for help in spite of how difficult and awkward it felt. Over time, as I became better at practicing Extreme Self-Care, I began to reclaim my life.

I've come to learn that overgiving is often a sign of deprivation—a signal that a need isn't being met, an emotion isn't being expressed, or a void isn't getting filled. For example, while you might dedicate hours to coordinating the family's social calendar, you may actually be yearning for deeper and more meaningful connections, stimulating conversation, or greater intimacy with yourself. You might also be available and generous with others because on some level you have an unconscious desire to get what you give, whether it's acknowledgment, affection, recognition, or support. Becoming aware of how and why you feel deprived can be a key to recognizing what needs to shift emotionally and physically to achieve Extreme Self-Care.

In what ways are you starving yourself of what you need to live a rich and fulfilling life? Since awareness in and of itself inspires change, I'd like to challenge you to spend the next 30 days becoming skilled at seeing the ways, big and small, that you deprive yourself of what you need. Rather than feel like a victim to something outside of yourself, when you realize that you alone are responsible for overgiving, you can actually empower yourself to do something about it. After all, no one else says yes, overbooks your schedule, or makes the needs of others a priority but you. The gift in owning this reality is that you own the power to change it, too.

To get an idea of what I mean, let's look at some common complaints and what they really mean:

— When you catch yourself saying things such as "I never have time to do what I want to do," **what you're really saying is:** "I don't take time for my needs."

— When you insist, "I always end up doing everything myself," **the truth of what you're really saying is:** "I don't ask for help."

— When you hear yourself complaining, "No one appreciates the things I do," **what you most likely mean is:** "I take on way too much, hoping that someone will notice and tell me how good I am or how grateful they are."

— And finally, when you use the excuse "My kids take up all of my time," **what you actually need to admit is:** "I've chosen to make my children's needs more of a priority than my own."

Extreme Self-Care Challenge: Discovering Where You Feel Deprived

Now it's your turn. This challenge is a call to consciousness—becoming more keenly aware of how, why, and where you feel deprived. For this exercise, I'd like you to buy a little notebook, one that will fit into your handbag or pocket. Then, every day this month, whenever you feel overwhelmed, frustrated, burdened, or resentful, stop and ask yourself:

- Where do I feel deprived?
- What do I need more of right now?
- What do I need less of?
- What do I want right now?
- What am I yearning for?
- Who or what is causing me to feel resentful and why?
- What am I starving for?

Get the idea? The choices you make either honor your Extreme Self-Care or they leave you feeling deprived. It's really that simple.

Your answers to these questions will help you identify the areas of your life that are calling for greater consciousness, an increase in your awareness of what needs to change to keep you from feeling deprived.

When you're doing this exercise, it's important that you're specific about your needs. So instead of writing: "I feel deprived because I have no time to myself," for instance, you might say: "I feel deprived of solitary, uninterrupted time away from my children and husband, which allows me to do something just for me, such as read a good novel, have lunch with a friend, or take a quiet bath." Being introspective and taking time to arrive at your answers thoughtfully will allow you to gain greater clarity about what your soul needs most to no longer feel deprived.

For example:

1. Instead of acknowledging that you need "to eat better," you may recall how particular foods make you feel, and recognize that you have more energy when you avoid meat or dairy products and consume more vegetables.

2. Rather than just saying that you need "fresh air," you might feel called to take "a brisk walk in nature every day in a place where I can breathe deep, feel at peace, and take in the surrounding beauty."

3. Instead of simply realizing that you "need help from others," be clear about the *kind* of help you need by jotting down something like: "I need someone to do the laundry every week, get the lawn mowed when I'm not around, and do some of the grocery shopping."

4. And rather than noting that you're "tired of directing staff meetings at work," you could write: "I need someone to run the staff meeting on Mondays, take notes, and then distribute them to the appropriate people."

Other needs might involve:

- Getting more (or better) sleep

- Developing a creative outlet

- Creating soul-nourishing friendships

- Considering ways to have more fun and/or adventure

- Identifying and seeking pleasurable activities and experiences

- Finding soul-nourishing space at home or at work

Becoming aware of how you experience deprivation in your life is critical to making the changes required to achieve optimal wellness and happiness. Keep your inner antenna finely tuned to what you need.

Resources

- *Get Out of Your Own Way: Overcoming Self-Defeating Behavior,* by Mark Goulston, M.D., and Philip Goldberg—to aid you in identifying and successfully dealing with self-sabotage.

- *The Drama of the Gifted Child: The Search for the True Self,* by Alice Miller—helps you reclaim your life by discovering your own crucial needs and your own truth.

- *The Dark Side of the Light Chasers: Reclaiming Your Power, Creativity, Brilliance, and Dreams,* by Debbie Ford—a wonderful book about owning and embracing all aspects of who we are, such as the overachiever, the caregiver, the martyr, and so on.

- *Eat, Pray, Love: One Woman's Search for Everything Across Italy, India, and Indonesia,* by Elizabeth Gilbert—a moving story of one woman's journey to find herself.

- The official Website of Alanis Morissette (**www.alanis.com**)—this remarkable woman produces inspiring music that chronicles the life journey we all take when we choose to live a more conscious life.

Chapter Two

Mirror, Mirror on the Wall

Several months ago, I was invited to be a guest on *The Oprah Winfrey Show* to talk about the Law of Attraction. Joining me onstage were Martha Beck, the author of *Finding Your Own North Star: Claiming the Life You Were Meant to Live;* and Louise Hay, the author of *You Can Heal Your Life* and the founder of Hay House, the publisher of this book. During the show, as we talked about using the power of the mind to direct the course of our lives, Louise repeatedly emphasized the importance of learning to love oneself as a prerequisite to attracting joy, abundance, wellness, meaningful experiences, and the like.

Over and over she suggested that, on a daily basis, audience members and viewers practice saying "I love you" when looking in the mirror. By the end of the show, I thought, *I need to pay attention to what she's talking about.*

At 82, Louise is a wise soul—a woman who's lived an extraordinary life that has inspired millions. I was moved and impressed by her conviction about the power of mirror work. After all, it speaks to the importance of self-love and self-acceptance, which I consider to be the foundation of Extreme Self-Care. So, right then and there, I made a decision to take Louise's advice to heart. I would start saying "I love you, Cheryl" each time I looked into a mirror every day for a month and see what happened.

∞

For most people, the idea of telling themselves "I love you" as they look in the mirror is a tricky exercise. The thought of doing so can feel awkward or silly. It's just not an easy thing to do. In fact, for several days after the show, I intended to practice Louise's suggestion, but I kept forgetting about it. Then one night before going to bed, I was washing my face when I remembered my intention. Finally, with the mirror in full view, I looked into my eyes and said, "I love you, Cheryl." Immediately I felt self-conscious, as if someone were watching. I tried it again and glanced away, feeling embarrassed. On my third

attempt, I found myself focusing on the wrinkles around my eyes, the hairs that needed to be plucked at the edges of my brows, and the way my skin seemed to sag a bit at my throat. *Great,* I thought. *My attempt at self-love has now turned into a critical assessment of my aging process.* I was failing miserably.

What's so silly about telling ourselves that we love ourselves? Why is it so difficult to do something that's seemingly so simple? Because looking at ourselves intently, especially into our eyes, is a profoundly intimate act. As often as we use a mirror to perform grooming or maintenance tasks, rarely do we ever stop to gaze into our eyes for longer than a few seconds. When we do, there's no hiding. Most of us come face-to-face with the truth that we've abandoned that person we see in the mirror. I know that as I stared into my own eyes and repeated the phrase "I love you, Cheryl," I had to confront the fact that the statement didn't ring true. The reality was that I saw flaws long before I felt love. And that's the point.

To practice Extreme Self-Care, you must learn to love yourself unconditionally, accept your imperfections, and embrace your vulnerabilities. From a spiritual perspective, it's about recognizing that you're a soul in a physical body who's here to learn to be more of who you really are. When you treat and view yourself with the respect you deserve, you experience the peace that comes from being present to yourself. The reason it's so hard to look deeply into your own eyes is because it forces the ego to step aside as you experience a moment of seeing your true nature: a spiritual being housed in a physical shell.

Mirror Work Works!

After hearing how serious Louise was about the mirror exercise and seeing what she'd created in her own life, I felt inspired to take it seriously, too. So for the next 30 days, I decided to stick with it—I wanted to see what would happen if I practiced it on a consistent basis. Every time I came in contact with a mirror, I would look into my eyes and say, "I love you, Cheryl." Whether I was washing my face, driving my car, trying on clothes in a dressing room, or looking at my reflection in my computer screen, I tried to look beyond the typical critical thoughts to the essence of who I was. By the third day, something interesting started to happen.

Each time I said "I love you, Cheryl," I felt a little less awkward and a little kinder toward myself. It still wasn't easy, but it was getting more comfortable. By the end of the first week, I noticed that the critical voices in my head had started to soften. When my mind drifted back to my flaws, I'd gently refocus my thoughts and remember that I was learning to love and accept myself rather than taking an inventory of what needed to change or improve. During the second week, this kinder, gentler perspective began

to radiate out into my daily life. I was becoming more patient with others as well as myself. I was now able to steer my mind to the present rather than worrying so much about the past or future. And I was less apt to push myself to do things I didn't want to do. *Hmm,* I thought, *maybe this exercise isn't so silly after all.*

As I continued the practice over that month, an internal shift occurred. I started to develop a deeper, more loving relationship with myself. I noticed that whenever something happened that was stressful or upsetting, it didn't bring me down so much or stay with me so long. Instead, I remained calm and steady . . . more able to find my center. When something frustrated me, I stopped feeding on the drama and just let it go. If someone said or did something hurtful, I spoke up right away. I also began to care more about what went into my mind and body, from avoiding depressing or violent news to choosing more nutritious food.

And as I kept on practicing the mirror exercise, I began to see a more loving part of me reflected in other areas of my life—places I hadn't considered or paid attention to before. For example, my husband and I had adopted a beautiful blue/gray Chartreux cat that we found at a shelter. As we grew to love this kitten we named "Poupon," I could see how I had changed. The way I treated Poupon was how I was learning to treat myself.

It's amazing how pets can help us see the love we have to give. It certainly has for me. When I'm with Poupon, I use a gentler, sweeter tone of voice. I love feeding him healthy meals and giving him fresh, clean water during the day. I always take the time—no matter how busy I am—to play with him and give him the attention, care, and exercise he needs. And if he does something wrong like break a glass or knock over a plant, I simply clean it up and patiently guide him away from the mess. I never berate him for making mistakes.

Just as my cat is a wonderful mirror for how I need to treat myself, you also have a mirror that reflects a more loving and tender side of you. Perhaps it's your child, grandchild, or garden—what you care for most, in a loving and patient way, holds clues to how you need to care for yourself more consistently.

The longer I used the mirror exercise, the more I began to see that an important shift was under way—a shift from good girl to good mother. On a fundamental level, that's what Extreme Self-Care is all about: extraordinary mothering. A good mother knows what helps a child feel whole in every way. She develops a finely tuned sensor that lets her know what her children need; and using a loving, discerning eye, does her best to meet these needs.

As I thought about the concept of being a good mother to oneself, I was reminded of an experience I had while teaching the concept of Extreme Self-Care at Kripalu, a retreat center located in the beautiful Berkshires of western Massachusetts. As I often do during my retreats, I played one of my favorite CDs—*Mother Divine,* by Kurt Van Sickle—a chant to help listeners quiet their busy minds during a meditation exercise. Just minutes after it started, several people began to cry. Looking around, I thought about the number of times I've watched this happen over the years. Time and again, as I played this particular music, men and women would be moved to tears.

Now, on this day, after the meditation came to an end, I waited several minutes before asking the group to talk about their experience. Many members commented that the music evoked a deep sadness—a longing for a connection to a maternal presence that would hold them, care for them, and provide them with comfort. Some spoke about a hunger for a kind of mothering they never received growing up. As I listened to their stories, I felt a deep sense of compassion for their pain. We all wanted and needed the same thing, and that's what Extreme Self-Care can provide for us: good mothering.

Extreme Self-Care Challenge: Falling in Love with You

While the idea of doing mirror work may seem more like a *Saturday Night Live* skit (remember

Al Franken's portrayal of Stuart Smalley?) than an act of self-love and acceptance, I challenge you to do it anyway. For each of the next 30 days, make a point to stand or sit in front of a mirror, look directly into your eyes, and repeat out loud, "I love you, [insert your first name]."

Regardless of how awkward or silly it feels, repeat it anyway. Repeat it until you begin to experience yourself in a spiritual way—as a presence that's deeper, broader, and more expansive than your physical self. Think of it as moving beyond the personality called "you" and connecting with yourself more deeply at the level of your soul. This experience does take time, so don't worry if it seems hard. You'll have an entire month to practice, and there's no need to rush. For now, just show up and allow yourself to get comfortable with this new level of connection and intimacy.

Resources

- *You Can Heal Your Life,* by Louise L. Hay—one of the early self-help books that's stood the test of time, telling the story of Louise's life and making the link between the mind and the body by using a practical reference list of physical ailments and their corresponding emotional triggers.

- *You Can Heal Your Life, the Movie*—an inspirational DVD that chronicles Louise's inspirational journey. It also features a number of luminaries in the fields of self-help, health, spirituality, and New Thought who discuss the power of our thoughts to influence the quality of our lives.

- *Mother Divine,* by Kurt Van Sickle—a great chanting CD to inspire good mothering.

- My CD *Tuning In: Listening to the Voice of Your Soul*—this will teach you to go within to access your own wisdom using a 10-, 20-, and 30-minute guided-meditation process.

- *A New Earth: Awakening to Your Life's Purpose,* by Eckhart Tolle—a life-changing work that will guide you to understand and perceive yourself as a spiritual being having a human experience.

Chapter Three

Let Me Disappoint You

I hate being disappointed. For me, getting my hopes up and then having them dashed is and has always been a very difficult thing to take. That's why when someone asks for a favor, my reflex is often to say yes when I'd really rather say no. Or I spend far too long devising a gracious excuse, only to end up feeling frustrated and resentful for having wasted so much of my time.

Not long after I started working with Thomas Leonard, he challenged me to do something that sent waves of anxiety coursing through my veins. He knew that I was too concerned with what people thought of me and that I was bending over backward to be liked. So, to help me get over my need to be a good girl, he suggested that I make one person angry every day for an entire month. His intention was to help me become "desensitized" to my fear of conflict and letting people down by confronting their anger, disappointment, or hurt feelings head-on. Just the thought of doing this made me sick to my stomach. And he knew it. But he (and eventually I) also knew that it was important. It helped me to start caring less about what others think and more about what *I* think. My willingness to face this fear paved the way for a more honest way of life.

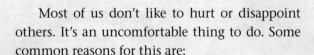

Most of us don't like to hurt or disappoint others. It's an uncomfortable thing to do. Some common reasons for this are:

> ❧ We don't want to feel guilty.
>
> ❧ We don't want to disappoint others because we know how bad it feels.

> ❧ We don't have the language to let someone down with grace and love.
>
> ❧ Our fear of conflict and our desire to keep the peace keep us from telling the truth.
>
> ❧ We want people to like us, and we feel uncomfortable when they don't.

One of the harsh realities about practicing Extreme Self-Care is that you must learn to manage the anxiety that arises when other people are disappointed, angry, or hurt. And they will be. When you decide to break your pattern of self-sacrifice and deprivation, you'll need to start saying no, setting limits, and putting boundaries in place to protect your time, energy, and emotional needs. This poses a difficult challenge for any sensitive, caring person. Why? Because you will, for instance, disappoint a friend when you decide not to babysit her kids. Or you'll probably hurt your son's feelings when you tell him that he has to walk to his friend's house instead of always being chauffeured. Or you might anger your partner when you ask him to wash his own clothes. Because you'll be changing the rules of the game, certain individuals won't like it. But remember, if you want to live a meaningful life that also makes a difference in the lives of others, you need to make a difference in your own life first. That way your motivation is pure and without regret.

How to Disappoint the Right Way

It's amazing to see what some people will do to avoid hurting or disappointing others. My conversation with Barbara, a woman who called in to my Internet radio show, illustrates this well.

Barbara was aware of her tendency to be a good girl, and even before she contacted me, she knew exactly what was going on. "I'm about to commit the ultimate good-girl act," she admitted. "For the last six months, my manager has worked hard to help me find a new position in a part of the country with a warmer climate, which is something I've wanted for a long time. But as I go through the interview process, it's becoming clear that the job isn't what I thought it would be, and I don't think I'll be happy. And here's the crazy thing—believe it or not, I'm actually thinking about taking the job anyway. Because my manager has really gone out of his way to help me, I'd hate to let him down."

As outrageous as this story seems, I wasn't surprised in the least. If you think about it, I'm sure you can recall times when you've done a similar thing. For example, even though everything

inside of you screamed "No!" perhaps you agreed to take on a new client just because you didn't want her to feel rejected. Or maybe you argued with your spouse about not having enough time together, and then you found yourself agreeing to run a fund-raiser for your child's school that very day, simply because you wanted the other parents to know how committed you were. Every day people make critical decisions based on what others want, knowing on some level that they're committing an act of self-betrayal. The role of the good girl (or boy) is a tough one to turn down.

So what happens when you start to let people down and they get upset? When you practice Extreme Self-Care there will be fallout, to be sure. In fact, you may lose some relationships that you thought were important to you. This is bound to happen, because if you tend to over-give, you've trained those in your life to expect it and they'll question you once you stop. Remember that by making your needs a priority, you're also changing the rules.

Don't be surprised if someone close to you—a best friend, family member, or spouse—tries to reel you back in by making more demands or tempting you with guilt. When this happens, the worst thing you can do is give in, as that sends mixed messages and teaches others to doubt your word. Instead, you need to be honest, direct, and resolved to take care of yourself. Don't over-explain, defend, or invite a debate about how you feel. The fewer words, the better.

This is why I emphasize having good support in place prior to starting the work outlined in this book. Left on your own to master the art of disappointment, it's almost a given that you'll let your guard down or lose some of your resolve. Don't allow this to happen—enlist some help. You'll need the assistance of those who are committed to their own Extreme Self-Care so that they can be your advocates as you take a stand for your life.

Having support makes it easier to tell and live your truth. For years I've called upon friends or staff members to help me let people down. I've done things like ask for support both before and after a tough conversation. Asking others to hold you up when you feel wobbly is smart.

It's now time to start being honest and direct, in a kind and loving way, with the people in your life so that you can stay focused on meeting your needs.

Here are some guidelines for staying strong while taking good care of yourself:

1. Buy some time. When someone makes a request of you, there are two things you should do. First, put space between the request and your answer. Before quickly responding, "Yes, I'm in!" take some time to consider the consequences of your response. Always say, "I'll need to get back to you," "I'll need to sleep on it," or "I need to check with someone before I commit" (even if that someone is you).

Second, let the person know *up front* that you may not be able to oblige. This makes it less personal. Statements such as "I've recently made a decision to limit the commitments I make, so I may not be able to do this" can take the pressure off should you decide that it's not in your best interest. Preparing people early on for the possibility that you won't be able to help them does something else as well. It encourages those who are asking for help to consider other options sooner rather than later.

2. Do a gut check. Once you've bought yourself some time, the next step is to check in to see if what's being requested is something you'd really like to do. Ask yourself: "On a scale from 1 to 10, how much do I really want to do this?" The closer your answer is to a 10, the more you should consider saying yes. If you're still not sure, ask yourself this: "If I knew this person wouldn't be angry, disappointed, or upset, would I say no?"

Over the years I've discovered that those who have a tendency to put the needs of others first commonly make *defensive decisions*. Rather than think about what *they* want to do, they immediately worry about what others need and how they might respond to hearing no. But practicing Extreme Self-Care means thinking about what *you* need first. Would satisfying this request bring you joy, fulfillment, or pleasure? Is it something you're not really thrilled to do, yet you know would support an important relationship? Let's face it, there will always be times when you do things you'd rather not just to be there for someone you love. Be certain, though, that you're doing it to show love or to strengthen your connection, not out of guilt and obligation—a strategy that can actually backfire and drive a wedge between you and the one you care about.

3. Tell the truth directly—with grace and love. In all my years of coaching, I've learned that one of the main reasons why people struggle with disappointing others or saying no is because they lack the language to do so with grace and love. The moment I help someone craft a caring and respectful response, his or her courage soars.

If we go back to Barbara's story (the woman who was considering the job transfer just to keep her manager happy), here's an example of how she could present a thoughtful, considerate no:

Bob, this is a tough conversation for me to have. I know how hard you've worked on my behalf to help me find a new job, and I'm deeply grateful. But the truth is that the more I learn about the position, the more I realize that it's not for me. I'm so appreciative of what you've done for me that I actually considered taking the job, but I couldn't do that to myself and I know it wouldn't be good

for the company. So I've decided to pass, but I want to thank you very much for your time and effort. Please let me know what I can do to help you maintain your relationship with your contact.

This example demonstrates three important steps to telling the truth with grace and love. They are:

— Be honest about how you feel without overexplaining yourself. Let the person know that you regret having to turn down the request (if it's true), but don't leave a door open when you need a wall. Be direct ("I feel bad about letting you down, but I need to") instead of wishy-washy ("I don't think I can do it, but if something changes, I'll let you know"). Allow your humanness to shine through, but don't give the impression that you're open to any discussion. The idea is to be considerate with your choice of words while sending a clear message that you need to say no.

— Tell the truth directly, plain and simple. Stick to one or two concise lines and explain (briefly), if need be, why you can't fulfill the request. Then move on to the next step.

— Depending on the circumstance, ask how you can support someone with an awkward situation or get them the help they need. However, do this *only* when you have an ethical responsibility that relates to a particular person or situation. For example, if you need to leave a volunteer position in the middle of a fund-raising campaign, you could recommend another person to take your place or help write an ad. Or if you promised to help your best friend paint her living room and then change your mind, you might do what you can to find someone to hire and then share in the cost.

Let's look at a few more examples where you can use this three-step plan:

Scenario #1: You're invited to the wedding of a friend who lives in another state, but you can't afford to go. Telling the truth with clarity, grace, and love might sound like this:

I wish I didn't have to, but I might end up hurting your feelings. I won't be able to attend your wedding and I'm sorry. My family can't afford the expense at this time, and since I hate to miss your big day, what can we do to acknowledge this special time in some other way?

Scenario #2: After agreeing to babysit your best friend's children for the weekend, you realize that you're late in finishing an important project at work. You need to spend the next few weekends catching up so you won't let the team down. Here's an idea of what to say:

I'm sorry to disappoint you, but something came up at work and I'm behind schedule on an important project. I'll get into trouble if I don't spend the next two weekends working on it, so I'll need to back out of my agreement to babysit the kids at the end of the month. I feel bad, and I'm wondering if we can put our heads together to help you find someone else.

Scenario #3: You've been asked to join the board of a local charity. Try this:

Thank you for your invitation. While I'm unable to accept, I wish you all the best with your organization [project, goals, or what have you].

This is a great way to offer a short, courteous, and direct response to the kind of professional requests or more general invitations that you instinctively know wouldn't be the right fit. After years of struggling with how to graciously decline requests, I've found that this one does the trick. There's no need to explain why—just tell the truth and genuinely wish them the best.

Finally, keep in mind that being honest about your commitment to self-care is almost always something people can hear, understand, and respect. So something like this would be ideal for just about any situation:

> In an effort to take care of myself and to spend more time at home, I need to decline your offer, although I'm honored that you asked.

Remember, if you're going to disappoint people the right way, the idea is to tell the truth with respect and care, not manage their emotions. While you can't control how someone feels or how they react, you *can* control how *you* feel and how you choose to make your point. Don't measure your success by the response you receive. Measure it by how you feel once your anxiety disappears. Do you know in your heart that you made the right decision? Do you feel relieved? Are you pleased with the way you handled saying no? Are you glad you did it? If the answers to these questions are yes, then you've done the right thing for everyone involved.

Extreme Self-Care Challenge: Learn to Use Your Voice

Now that you have the tools you need to protect your energy, you're ready to practice saying no and to take good care of yourself. Over the next 30 days, become a master at using your voice. Your goal is to get comfortable with disappointing people, facing conflict, dealing with anger, and realizing the possibility that you might hurt someone's feelings. Use what you learned in this chapter to handle requests in a healthier way. Then each time you decline a request, use the experience as a learning opportunity by writing about it in your notebook or journal.

As you think about what happened, ask yourself:

🪷 What did I do that I feel good about?

🪷 What language did I use to state my position? What worked best?

🪷 What would I do differently the next time I'm faced with a request?

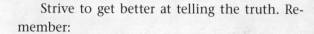

Strive to get better at telling the truth. Remember:

- Always take your time before responding.

- Always do a gut check—be conscious of the way you *feel*.

- Tell the truth with grace and love, in a clear and decisive way

Resources

- My book *Stand Up for Your Life*—shows you how to develop the courage and confidence to make choices that honor your values, needs, and desires.

- *My Answer Is No . . . If That's Okay with You: How Women Can Say No and (Still) Feel Good About It,* by Nanette Gartrell, M.D.—a practical guide to setting boundaries while preserving important relationships.

- *Difficult Conversations: How to Discuss What Matters Most,* by Douglas Stone, Bruce Patton, and Sheila Heen—one of the best guides I've found for facing conflict.

- SelfGrowth.com (**www.selfgrowth.com**)—this Website is dedicated to providing valuable information on personal growth as it relates to success, relationships, health, money, spirituality, and so forth.

- Helpguide (**www.helpguide.org**)—an online resource for empowering you and your loved ones to understand, prevent, and resolve life's challenges.

Chapter Four

The Power of Rhythm and Routine

I love the ocean. My perfect day is spent riding waves at the beach, preferably early in the morning or just before sunset, when the light is beautiful and the crowds are sparse. I've loved the ocean my whole life. Some of my greatest memories are of piling in the station wagon with my family for a long drive to the beach, where we'd spend the day swimming, playing in the sand, digging for clams, or combing the shore for shells. I've always been taken by the majesty of the sea; the mystery of the unseen world below; and the calming, rhythmic sound of the waves.

As I've often told readers and audiences, the beach is where I go for sanity, strength, and spiritual connection. I know that a quiet, meditative walk along the water will clear my head, lift my mood, and give me access to wisdom and insight rather than the misguided musings of my thinking mind. I also go there to feel more connected to God; the yearnings of my soul; and what I need to live an authentic, passionate life. In many ways, the ocean is my church.

Over the years, I've thought a lot about what draws people to the sea. I've walked by hundreds of men and women who were deep in thought as they ran or walked along the shore. I've stood with strangers—beach-loving brothers and sisters—to watch wild waves, 20 feet high, pound the shoreline in a winter storm. And I've spent countless hours with friends and fellow wave riders floating in the arms of Mother Nature, looking for the next big ride. To me, the ocean represents stability, strength, and a sense of peace and comfort that comes from consistent ebb and flow. When I spend time at the beach and in the water, I feel restored, reconnected to my core, and grounded in a way that spills over into my everyday life.

There's something healing about repetition and rhythm, and when I experience this in my everyday life, I feel centered and balanced. I was reminded of this during a time when I felt extremely overwhelmed. I was juggling several big projects, and every day seemed like one long, frustrating attempt to get to the important things I really wanted to do. Obligations, e-mails, phone calls, or requests all took up so much time that by the end of my workday, I had no time left for myself. Fed up with feeling so out of control, I decided to address the problem by using a simple yet powerful coaching technique.

I sat quietly, took a few deep breaths, and asked myself a challenging question: "What *one* thing can I do to make better use of my time so I completely eliminate the reason I feel so overwhelmed?"

After waiting several minutes, I had a surprising thought: *Get to sleep by 11 P.M. and get up by 7 A.M. every day.* Not an answer I expected. For quite some time, my sleep schedule had been a bit erratic due to traveling. I'm sensitive to jet lag, and I also like to stay up late when the world seems quiet enough to get important projects completed without interruptions. This would have been fine except for the fact that my schedule often required me to be up for meetings during the earlier part of the day. Burning the candle at both ends had made me edgy, anxious, and angry (both at myself and at the situation). No wonder I felt overwhelmed.

Because I've learned to trust my gut when it comes to things like this, I decided to change my sleep schedule for one month and see how it affected my life. The very next day, sitting in my office at 7:30 A.M., I felt better. There's something stimulating, almost magical, about the energy of early morning. I love the quiet and peacefulness, and the rising sunlight inspires my creativity.

One month later, during a time when I wasn't traveling, I realized that by sticking to my new routine, my life had more rhythm and flow, and it felt good. I was more productive and energized during the day, not to mention more focused, and my mood reflected the balance and consistency I'd created in my life. I soon found it easy to spend more time on the things that mattered most.

Riding Life's Waves

Finding a wavelike rhythm and routine reaps great rewards and can actually be a surprisingly powerful act of Extreme Self-Care. Routine adds stability to our lives and helps us feel more secure. It also provides much-needed relief from mentally managing too many responsibilities.

If you stop to think about it, you'll probably find that you already have some established routines in place, such as:

- Meeting your buddies for a weekly pickup soccer game

- Having your hair done regularly by the same stylist at the same salon

- Putting your kids to bed and getting them up at the same time every day

- Going to the gym every Monday, Wednesday, and Friday

- Scheduling your work meetings at the same time each week

- Walking the dog or feeding the cat at the same time every day

These routines become the rhythms by which you live and plan your life. And the benefits often affect you in ways you might not expect. For example, when you go to sleep and wake up at the same time every day, you support your body's adrenal system by keeping your hormones stable and balanced. A balanced body helps you create a balanced mind. As a result, peace and order begin to replace the chaos and frenetic energy of a busy life. Meeting with friends at the same time each week—be it having lunch with co-workers or working out with your pals at the gym—gives you a sense of connection and community that feels meaningful and fulfilling.

Think about the cycles of nature: seasons change, the sun rises and sets every day, and tides flow in and out. Unfortunately, our natural human rhythms are too often interrupted by busy lives. We eat at all hours of the day and night. We barely get enough sleep. And we're distracted by noise, making it nearly impossible to create regular, undisturbed periods that allow us to focus our energy and attention on one thing at a time. When we're not in our natural "flow," our mind and body get confused, which can cause a whole host of problems. For example, our ability to concentrate is disrupted, our moods shift dramatically throughout the day, our energy levels wax and wane, or our natural process of digestion and elimination gets interrupted or impaired.

Establishing a more balanced and healthy routine might mean doing one of the following at the same time every day:

- 🍃 Going to bed

- 🍃 Waking up

- 🍃 Exercising

- 🍃 Meditating

- 🍃 Eating breakfast, lunch, and/or dinner

- 🍃 Playing with or walking your pet

- 🍃 Writing in a journal or notebook

- 🍃 Going for a walk

- 🍃 Spending time with a loved one

Creating routines at work is also a very effective way to increase performance and productivity. Scheduling activities at the same time each week—meetings, uninterrupted work time, or visits with clients—creates a sense of order that gives the mind a much-needed rest. Setting up regular periods of time when you're not disturbed will give you a chance to get work done without energy-zapping distractions.

Other ways to create new rhythms on the job include:

- 🍃 Taking some time every morning to plan your day, rather than just diving in

- 🍃 Checking voice mail or e-mail at predetermined times throughout the day

- 🍃 Scheduling weekly meetings at the same time (this helps employees benefit from the power of routine, too!)

- 🍃 Giving yourself 20 minutes before you leave to tie up the day's loose ends

If you currently feel that you're not organized or grounded, there's a good chance that the peace of mind you long for lies in your ability to create a natural rhythm in your life. So let's get to it!

Extreme Self-Care Challenge: Finding Your Own Rhythm and Routine

This month is about experiencing the power of rhythm and routine. To get started, sit quietly and take several deep breaths. Then ask yourself the following question: "What one routine could I put in place this month that would improve my life the most?"

Notice the first thing that comes to mind (especially if it's something you'd like to ignore). Once you've identified what it is, put it in writing on a 3" x 5" index card and keep it in view throughout the month to remind you of your commitment.

Next, make a plan to put this routine in place for the next 30 days. For example, if you decide that you'll meditate for ten minutes in the morning, let family members know that you shouldn't be disturbed. Or if you plan to return work phone calls from 2:00 to 4:00 in the afternoon, be sure to let the appropriate people know (such as staff, clients, and so on).

Once your new routine has been in place for a week, take some time to consider how it has affected your emotional and physical well-being by answering the following questions:

- Are you more relaxed?

- Do you feel less overwhelmed?

- Are you more productive?

- Does your life seem more balanced?

Reinforce your new habit by keeping track of positive results in your notebook or journal throughout the month.

Resources

🌿 *SonicAid: Scientifically Designed Music to Help You Live Better* (4-CD set), by Dr. Lee Bartel (available through **www.brookstone.com**)—beautiful music for restful sleep, concentration, creativity, and relaxation.

🌿 *Chicken Soup for the Ocean Lover's Soul: Amazing Sea Stories and Wyland Artwork to Open the Heart and Rekindle the Spirit,* compiled by Jack Canfield, Mark Victor Hansen, and Wyland—a collection of stories from around the world that celebrate the magic of the ocean.

🌿 *Chicken Soup for the Beach Lover's Soul: Memories Made Beside a Bonfire, on the Boardwalk, and with Family and Friends,* compiled by Jack Canfield, Mark Victor Hansen, Patty Aubery, and Peter Veqso—a volume filled with recollections of special moments that will be appreciated by anyone who's been mesmerized by the spell of the sea.

🌿 *The Harvard Medical School Guide to a Good Night's Sleep,* by Lawrence Epstein, M.D., with Steven Mardon—a six-step plan for overcoming sleep problems.

Chapter Five

Take Your Hands off the Wheel

It all started with the dishwasher. After a good night's sleep, I walked into the kitchen one morning to make a cup of tea and found my husband loading dirty dishes into the top rack. I stood by quietly, taking special note of how he "tossed" them in without much concern for how they were placed. Once he was done and safely in his office, I—knowing full well that the dishwasher needed to be loaded *correctly*—walked over, opened the front of the machine, and proceeded to rearrange what he had done.

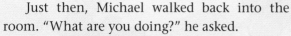

Just then, Michael walked back into the room. "What are you doing?" he asked.

"Nothing," I replied, looking guilty.

"No, really, what are you doing?" he demanded.

I quickly explained how important it was to put the items in the dishwasher in a certain way to ensure that they'd be cleaned properly.

Before I could finish my well-honed argument, he exclaimed, "That's ridiculous! They'll get clean regardless of how you put them in. Why don't you just tell the truth? Since I didn't do it *your* way, you need to fix it."

I felt like a little girl caught in the act of stealing candy at the corner store. I stood there, head bent, looking down at my slippers.

"Cheryl, what do you think goes through my mind when I come into the kitchen and find you redoing what I just did?"

I looked up with a sheepish grin on my face.

"It makes me think, *Why bother? It's never right, and she's just going to do it over anyway,*" Michael explained. "So I don't help out, and that's why you end up complaining that you never get the support you need. Rather than *receive* my help, you criticize it."

Ouch. I hate when you're face-to-face with the person who knows you better than anyone else in the world and there's nowhere to hide. Michael was right—I was a control freak.

Like so many women, my natural default is to want to be in charge by doing things myself.

And over time, this "I'll do it myself" mentality has turned into "Hi, I'm General Manager of the Universe, and you need to do this my way and in my time to keep me happy." What follows from there isn't pretty. Eventually I proudly wear the cloak of martyr, and everyone pays the price. I get bitchy and resentful, and I end up feeling painfully alone.

If there's one thing I've struggled with the most over the years as I've worked hard to become a more conscious woman, it's asking for *and* receiving help. Right now, standing in the kitchen with my husband, I was getting an automatic "F" in that subject.

There are plenty of reasons why we don't ask for help. First and foremost, those of us who like to be the boss have typically been in that role for a very long time. As a result, it doesn't even occur to us to ask. Second, there are the perceived costs. When I talk to people about why they don't ask for help, I hear things such as:

- "I don't want to appear weak."

- "It takes too much energy to explain what I need, so I don't bother."

- "I hate being disappointed when people don't follow through."

🌿 "It's too much of a hassle to fight with family members who resist helping out."

🌿 "I don't want to hear no."

🌿 "I don't want to feel indebted to anyone."

🌿 "When I'm at work, I know I can do it faster, cheaper, and better; so I don't want to waste time and money."

🌿 "In my family, we were taught to be self-sufficient, and I'm too proud to put anyone out."

If you look closely, you'll see that what all of these examples have in common is, in fact, control—the desire to avoid conflict or disappointment, or the attempt to manage the perceptions of others by not appearing weak. And then there's the idea that doing everything on your own makes you less indebted to others.

In the long run, the need to be in control and to do everything yourself can have unexpected consequences. I learned this lesson during a conversation with my best friend, Max, a soul sister who has taught me plenty about living a spiritually sane life.

Max had been going through a tough time dealing with an all-too-common and very painful situation: a mother who was diagnosed with dementia. As I'm sure many of you can imagine (or know from personal experience), a parent with dementia throws one's life into turmoil. There's the enormous amount of energy that goes into dealing with the diagnosis—researching treatment options, finding the right caregivers, locating an appropriate place for him or her to live, or managing the financial resources. Then there's the emotional cost when you're faced with the reality that you've now become a parent to your parent.

As we discussed the situation, Max told me something very important: "I now realize why we need to let go of control and allow others to take on some of the responsibility of handling life situations. Since my dad died many years ago, my older sister had always managed my mother's care, and now that she's gone [Max had lost her only sibling to cancer], I'm left to start from scratch. Had my sister shared the burden with me, I would have gained valuable knowledge and experience that would make this current situation easier to handle."

Later that day, I thought about our conversation and how it related to my own life. Where was I hanging on to control to the detriment of others? One answer came to mind immediately. Since I managed all of the finances for my family, I needed to share some of that responsibility with Michael so that he'd be able to easily take over should something happen to me.

How about you? Where are you holding tight to the wheel? What would others struggle with if you weren't around to handle it? Maybe it's time to start delegating more to the people you supervise at work. Or it might be wise to ease up on your tendency to micromanage others so they feel more valued and respected for their contributions.

When you let go of control and allow others to take the wheel, you empower them. You teach them to trust themselves, to become resourceful, and to take greater responsibility for the quality of their own lives. You can practice letting go in simple ways, like permitting your child to choose his or her own clothes for school; allowing a friend to navigate directions without butting in; or sharing household responsibilities with a teenager, like doing the laundry or cooking meals. You might even consider more challenging steps, like turning over the handling of the finances to your partner for a while, or insisting that a sibling contribute to the care of an elderly parent.

Allowing others to help means learning to surrender to the reality that there will be mistakes made and that things will not always get done your way. That's how people learn and grow. After all, think about how you came to handle what you do so well now. Chances are you made plenty of mistakes along the way and had to find your

own path, too. If you're used to being in charge, you'll need to keep letting go of the wheel when you're tempted to take back control, especially when the situation's not going according to your plans. Let others drive for a while—even though they may take a different road.

There are other consequences to attempting to do everything ourselves in an effort to maintain control. We often wound our most important relationships. We become critical and overbearing with loved ones, causing them to feel inadequate, frustrated, or incapable of handling even the simplest tasks. We may take family members for granted, expecting that they'll wait "one more minute" while we get something done. And over time, we lose the vital energy we need to experience pleasure and physical intimacy with our partners.

Sex and the Housekeeper

My client Jake was a bright and ambitious guy. He'd been married to his wife, Emily, for more than ten years, and they had two young boys and a busy home life. Emily also managed the office for Jake's marketing consulting firm, which he'd started early on in their marriage. They had a great relationship . . . that is, when they could find the time to spend together.

During one of our coaching sessions, Jake talked about the frustration he felt at not having

enough quality time with his wife. "I'm so busy at work—and she's so busy running the office, taking care of the house, and driving the kids to their activities—that we rarely see each other," he told me.

Since this wasn't the first time I'd heard him complain about the problem, I decided to challenge him to do something about it. "Tell me, Jake," I said, "what one thing could you take off of Emily's plate that would free her up to feel more relaxed and make her more available to you?"

As he considered my request, I immediately had an idea: "Why don't you hire a housekeeper to come in once a week to clean and do the laundry? That would certainly free up a lot of her time and energy."

Jake agreed that it would take a load off of his wife's shoulders, but he didn't think she'd go for it because "she likes things done her way and has a tough time giving up control."

I certainly knew that drill, so I pushed a little further. "Well, here's something to think about: would you like more sex?"

I smiled as I watched my question register on his face. He glanced away shyly for a moment, and then his eyes lit up like a Christmas tree. "Of course!" he replied. "Wouldn't most guys?"

"Then do whatever you have to do to convince Emily that you're hiring a housekeeper," I challenged. "Do the homework for her. Get referrals from neighbors, find a bonded service company, or do research on the Web. Just make sure you find someone good who's open to feedback and anxious to help. If you do that, trust me—you'll not only have more time together, you'll enjoy greater intimacy and more sex."

"Okay," Jake agreed enthusiastically. "I'm on it!"

I've met many women like Jake's wife who feel overburdened and short on support, and they tell me that sex becomes just another item on an already long to-do list. They feel driven to check off items on this list so that they can relax. And, when they finally do feel ready to relax, sleep is a far more appealing option.

When you feel pressed for time, overwhelmed with responsibilities, and alone with your misery, you repeatedly engage the body's "fight or flight" system, which raises your cortisol levels. This "alert mode" causes you to worry, to ruminate about what needs to get done, and to live in a chronic state of anxiety. Can you imagine enjoying the pleasure of lovemaking when your body is screaming, "Hurry up! I've got lots to do before I can stop worrying about today and start thinking about tomorrow!"? Of course not. You're ready for action, all right, but not the kind that welcomes intimacy.

Yet the intimacy that comes from a strong, healthy relationship is an important component of Extreme Self-Care. We all need physical closeness to feel deeply connected to our partners. So if a lack of sex or physical affection is an issue in your relationship, one of the first things you want to do is delegate the less important tasks of life and allow your body to relax. Hire someone else to clean your house or do the grocery shopping. I always tell my clients who feel starved for affection that if you want a woman to move closer, take something off her plate. As one good friend told me, "When my husband vacuums the house, it's as good as foreplay."

Several weeks after my conversation with Jake, we met for breakfast to catch up. My client had done his homework, and he and his wife had, in fact, hired a great housekeeper who also ended up babysitting their children now and then. "Now that you have more time together, are you having fun?" I asked him.

"You bet!" he said with a sly grin.

Letting Go

After years of arguing over household chores, my husband and I finally came up with a strategy that allowed me to let go of control so I could get the support I needed. I set up a form on my computer entitled "Things You Can Do to Support Me." At the end of the day, I'd list several things I didn't feel like doing or couldn't get to around the house. (At the end of the list, I always included one last item: "Kiss me when you come to bed.") Because Michael was a night owl, he usually tackled the to-do list after I fell asleep.

I still remember the first morning when I woke up and went into my office. There on my desk was the list with every item checked off. *Sure,* I thought, *we'll see how long this lasts.*

Over the course of the next few months, every time I left a list for my husband, I'd wake up to find it completed or with an explanation as to why a task hadn't yet been done. I was amazed that something that had been so contentious between us had been resolved with a simple list.

When I brought up this fact to Michael, he responded, "For years I've been telling you that I needed you to write things down, but you never listened. I can't read your mind, Cheryl, and I know I work better with a plan. When you leave me a list, it lets me know that you need help, it allows me to contribute, and I feel a sense of accomplishment. I was so used to your handling everything that I honestly never knew when you needed help, let alone what needed to be done. Now I'm relieved to be able to do something *before* you get overwhelmed and resentful. Trust me, it's much better for our relationship."

His last point was key. Now that we had a system in place for getting me the support I needed, I had no one to blame but myself when I suddenly felt resentful. As soon as Michael heard me complain about all I had to do, his response was always, "Where's the list?" I can't tell you how many times I was confronted with my controlling, "Lone Ranger" behavior. Why hadn't I done a list? Why wasn't I asking for help before I desperately needed it?

Whether you ask for help from a partner or spouse, your kids, or someone who works for you, learning to make a "Things You Can Do to Support Me" list will force you to get in the habit of thinking about where and when you need help *before* you feel like you're going to lose your mind.

Mastering the art of letting go of control and receiving help is important for several reasons:

1. You can't possibly live a life of Extreme Self-Care without assistance from others. Life just gets busier and more complicated all the time, and the more you try to do everything yourself, the more exhausted and resentful you'll feel.

2. The resentment you feel at having to do everything yourself will slowly eat away at your most precious relationships.

3. Your children need to learn how to ask for help, and the best way to teach them this skill is to become a role model.

4. It's great to share the wealth with others. When you hire someone—

a housekeeper, an assistant, a painter, or a plumber, for instance— remember that you're providing income to another family.

So how do you know when support is long overdue? Here are a few warning signals:

- You hear yourself chronically complaining about how much you have to do.

- You feel like the weight of the world is resting squarely on your back.

- You fantasize about packing a bag and leaving for the nearest deserted island.

- You find yourself crying at unexpected times and in unexpected places (or you feel like you need a good cry).

- You start yelling at inanimate objects or at drivers in front of you who are driving the speed limit.

- You're so exhausted that the idea of brushing your teeth feels like too much work.

These are clues that you need someone to lean on—*now*. Sure, I know that asking for and receiving help is challenging. Many of us use the same arguments: "No one can do it better than I can," "It takes too much time to explain what needs to be done," or "It's just easier to do it myself." And while I've used these same excuses, I've also learned to remind myself that there's too much at stake. The quality of my life is directly related to the quality of how present I am to it, and that's far more important than completing any task.

But be warned! When we finally decide that we'll let go of the wheel and allow someone else to help, it can be quite comical to see how we prevent ourselves from receiving. For example, you might ask your busy brother who keeps promising to fix the leak in your basement to do so, even though you know that he'll never get around to doing it. That way you can say, "See, no one follows through for me." Or you may expect perfection when you hire a new assistant and end up watching him like a hawk, pouncing on a mistake just so you can prove yourself right. I've even seen a friend reluctantly hire a housekeeper who didn't clean the way she wanted, and instead of giving her feedback about what needed to change, she simply fired her. It was much easier to fall back on the belief that no one could do it better than she could than to face her fear of asking for what she needed.

At this stage of the game, the only way to create a successful life based on your values and deepest longings (let alone the only way to maintain your sanity), is to take your hands off the wheel and become masterful at asking for and receiving help. You cannot manage your home, care for your personal needs, honor your emotional and physical health, be successful at work, or be the kind of parent you hope to be without the support of others. Period.

Extreme Self-Care Challenge: Learn to Ask for and Receive Help

Okay, it's time to get to work on this month's challenge. The goal is to practice letting go so others can take the wheel. We'll use the "Things You Can Do to Support Me" list as a strategy for mastering this skill.

Pick an area of your life, be it home or work, where you could use the most aid. Then choose the person (or persons) you'd like help from and explain how the list works. Let this person know that you're ready to let go of control and you'd like his or her assistance.

Negotiate how you'll work with the list by considering the following areas:

- How many items will you include on the list?

- Where will you leave it?

🍃 When would you like to have these items completed by?

🍃 What should your support person do when he or she can't meet a deadline?

🍃 Who will ultimately be in charge if additional help is needed?

As you begin to use the list, be sure to give your support person permission to let you know when you're trying to take back control—when you start to do something you've asked him or her to do or when you're interfering in the process. It's also very important to let him or her make mistakes. Keep in mind that just because something isn't done your way, that doesn't mean it's wrong. And sure, mistakes will be made, but they're rarely life threatening. When given room to breathe, people generally bring their best selves to the task at hand.

Good luck!

Resources

🌿 Beliefnet (**www.beliefnet.com**)—a Website dedicated to helping visitors find and walk a spiritual path that will bring them comfort, hope, clarity, strength, and happiness. Great faith-inspired information for those times when you need to surrender and trust that all will be well.

🌿 Assist U (**www.assistu.com**)—Stacy Brice, a pioneer who founded the profession of "virtual assistants" (or VAs), offers this site as both a training resource for VAs, as well as a referral service to find your own virtual assistant.

🌿 *Mayday!: Asking for Help in Times of Need,* by M. Nora Klaver—takes a look at why we don't ask for help, why we should, and how to do it.

🌿 *Help Is Not a Four-Letter Word: Why Doing It All Is Doing You In,* by Peggy Collins, with Deborah Saverance—shows you how to recognize the signs of burnout; ease the demands you put on yourself; and start enjoying your work, your family, and your life.

🌿 Merry Maids (**www.merrymaids.com**)—if you're ready to hire a housekeeper, this Website has great resources.

Chapter Six

The Absolute No List

Ever since the publication of my first book, *Take Time for Your Life*, I've often been referred to as an expert in work/life balance— a life coach who helps people find some sanity in their busy lives. As a result, people who feel overworked, overburdened, or under pressure ask me to share time-management secrets, or strategies for being better organized, so they can get a handle on their chaotic schedules. My response is always the same: "You can't make sanity out of an insane situation."

The truth is this: if your life is chaotic, your schedule is overcrowded, and your brain is too full to think straight, the key to reclaiming your life has a lot more to do with what you *remove* from your life than how you organize it. And from what I've seen, most people need to remove at least 30 percent of what they have on their plates just to get started.

It was in my first book that I introduced the concept of Extreme Self-Care that Thomas Leonard had shared with me all those years ago. One of the most immediate ways to feel the effects of this level of care is to become very discriminating about how you spend your precious time and energy, so I offered an exercise in the book called the "Absolute Yes list" that became quite popular with readers. It asked them to think carefully about their top priorities, such as their emotional, physical, or spiritual health; their children and other significant relationships; community service; work-related projects; and so forth.

Once readers had identified what most needed their immediate attention, I asked them to choose their top-seven priorities—those things they would devote their time and attention to over a three- to six-month period. Once they narrowed the list down to seven, I then had them write these priorities on a 3" x 5" index card that they could keep in view. By referring to their Absolute Yes list, readers would ensure that their precious time and energy would first and foremost be devoted to the things that mattered most.

Over the years, I was often surprised to discover that most people neglected to include themselves—that is, their own care—on the list. As a matter of fact, I was once booed by audience members at *The Oprah Winfrey Show* when I suggested that mothers needed to put their self-care at the top of their list, ahead of the needs of their children. While I understood their reaction, I knew from coaching plenty of adults that the effects of being raised by a mother who neglected her needs—and consequently often carried internal rage because her needs weren't met—would be painful.

The effects of being raised by someone who harbors these unexpressed feelings can be seen in everything from the fear of having more success than a parent to conflict phobia or keeping peace at any cost. And this lack of modeling good self-care just continues the legacy of deprivation. I've traveled a long road relaying the message that the greatest gift a mom can give a child is making her needs a top priority. We need to put the idea of "self-care as selfish" behind us for good.

After *Take Time for Your Life* was published, I found that the Absolute Yes list inspired many people, including myself, to begin using this exercise in another way—by asking the question, "Is this an absolute yes?" when making decisions. Over time it became a litmus test I used when making all kinds of choices: whether or not to accept a speaking engagement or hire a new employee, or even in choosing a restaurant to visit. If it wasn't an absolute yes, then it was a no.

The list's next evolution is what this chapter is about. Yes, knowing what's an absolute yes is important—but so is knowing what's an absolute no. As you practice Extreme Self-Care, you'll gradually raise your standards for what you will and will not tolerate in your life. As a result, you'll find that there are certain things you used to do that no longer honor the level of self-care you now need to be your best.

For example, for years I used to be available by phone or computer at all times during the day and into the night. But these days, Extreme Self-Care means protecting my energy and my nervous system. So now I keep the ringers turned off on the phones in my home and office; I don't have voice mail on my cell phone; and I rarely, if ever, take e-mail on the road. I want to protect my emotional and mental health. After all, I want to live my life, not rush through it.

Think about the things you no longer do, or would like to stop doing, in order to protect your precious energy and to honor your values. Maybe you're tired of being responsible for cooking every meal, and you're ready to allow your teenagers to learn a new skill. You've done your job, and it's just not an absolute yes anymore. Maybe you'd like to enjoy a Sunday afternoon

to yourself rather than attend a weekly dinner with your extended family. It's not how you want to spend your time right now, so it's a no. Or maybe you're no longer willing to have lunch with colleagues who pick your brain. While it used to be okay to freely share your great ideas, it's now turned into an absolute no.

The concept of creating a list of absolute noes is important. It serves as a potent reminder of what you no longer do so that you can protect your quality of life. It can be eye-opening and helpful to read about what others consider an absolute no, especially if you have trouble creating your own list. That's why I asked several friends to share their examples. As you read through them, notice how they make you feel, and put a check mark next to the ones that you'd like to adopt.

My Absolute No List: I No Longer . . .

 Rush.

 Jump out of bed in the morning. I give myself the time and space I need to start the day in a serene and relaxed state.

 Live without pets.

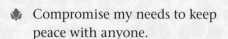

- Compromise my needs to keep peace with anyone.

- Eat meat.

- Balance my accounts and pay the bills—I have someone else do it.

- Argue with people who see debating as a sport.

- Use my credit cards unless I can pay them off in full at the end of the month.

- Keep anything in my home that I don't love or need.

- Keep my mouth shut when someone is out of line.

- Go to events that require hours of idle chitchat.

- Tolerate, or participate in, gossip.

- Deal with difficult life situations alone.

- Hire anyone—be it a lawyer, doctor, health-care provider, or what have you—who treats me with disrespect.

- Take phone calls during meals.

- Accept verbal abuse from a boss or co-worker.

- Go to work when I'm sick.

- Keep my opinions to myself when they don't align with those of others in the room.

- Let social norms dictate what I should be interested in, whether it's clothes, art, music, or the like. I love what I love.

- Invest time in relationships that aren't aligned with who I am and who I want to be.

- Accept wasteful packaging at restaurants, stores, and so on.

- Finish reading books that lose my interest.

- Take junk mail into my home (I have a recycling box outside my door).

- Feel the need to check my e-mail multiple times a day.

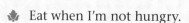

- Eat when I'm not hungry.

- Get caught up in other people's drama.

- Feel an obligation to spend time with family members or friends who choose to live in chaos.

- Feel bad about saying no when no is what's best for me.

- Let my mind be on work when I'm not working.

- Let the TV networks dictate when I watch my favorite shows (I record what I want to see and then watch it at my leisure).

- Have my e-mail program set to automatically receive new messages. I choose when I get my mail.

- Keep clothes I hope to fit into "someday."

- Throw away anything that can be recycled.

- Buy cars that aren't fuel efficient.

- Spend time with people who talk *at* me instead of *with* me.

The preceding are great examples of how the rules change as we incorporate the practice of Extreme Self-Care into our lives. When I share these ideas with clients or workshop members, I get a variety of reactions. Some are inspired to set new limits in their own lives, while others are surprised and a bit intimidated to think that they could actually live by some of these rules. Then there are those who get agitated because they can't see the possibility for their own lives, they can't afford to pay for someone else to do something they no longer want to do, or they aren't yet where they feel deserving of such standards.

Fortunately, all of these obstacles can be overcome. One small "no" can open your mind to new possibilities. Trading services with others can tackle financial hurdles. Or raising your standards in even one area of your life can increase your feeling of deservedness.

All of these reactions are a normal part of the process as we go about the business of upgrading our lives. One of the most common reactions from women after hearing the aforementioned examples is: "A lot of these seem like they belong to someone with a sense of entitlement, and I couldn't possibly be that self-important." While I remember feeling the same way early in my journey, I can assure you that, if anything, most of the good men and women who show up for coaching or at my speaking engagements need to develop a *stronger* sense of entitlement when it comes to taking better care of their needs.

It's also important to note that some of the examples demonstrate the power that practicing Extreme Self-Care has on others. Choosing not to accept wasteful packaging at a restaurant, refusing to participate in gossip, or buying a fuel-efficient car are all examples of how good self-care turns into caring for others.

The Absolute No list you create will tell you a lot about yourself. If you can't think of anything, for example, it could mean that you need to put your needs on the front burner. If your list only has two or three items, then it may be time to give more consideration to what needs to change in your life. And if you look at your list and feel good about the rules you live by—the ones that protect you and keep you strong—then it might be time for a celebration.

Starting your own list is an important step in learning about where you fall on the self-care spectrum. Let's get going. . . .

Extreme Self-Care Challenge: Create Your Own Absolute No List

The first thing you'll want to do is spend a week looking for those activities you no longer do, no longer want to do, or would like to give up at some point in the future. In addition, pay attention to the sources of frustration in your life—the same old arguments, the typical commitments you make that backfire, or the situations that always leave you feeling drained or resentful. If you're tired of volunteering your services to makeshift organizations that don't have their acts together, for instance, this is important information to know when developing your Absolute No list. You'll want to add something like "I no longer volunteer for any organization that doesn't have a concrete vision, plan, and sufficient staffing" to your Absolute No list.

When looking for absolute noes, pay close attention to how you feel in your body. Look for those times when you feel tension in your neck or shoulders, tightness in your arms, aching in your head, or butterflies in your stomach. For example, if you feel edgy and short-tempered every time tax season rolls around because of the work involved in preparing your returns, it may be time to stop doing them. You'll want to add this to your list: "I no longer prepare my own taxes. I pay someone else to do it."

Next, look back over the examples in your notebook and use them to begin creating your own Absolute No list. Don't forget to go back through the examples mentioned earlier in this chapter so that you can include the ones you checked off as well. Start a file on your computer or develop a handwritten list in your notebook that captures what you've learned during the first week.

Finally, post your list in a place where you'll see it every day for at least the next month, and be sure to take five or ten minutes each day to read through it. As you do, imagine installing these new rules into your brain like a self-care software upgrade—a program that will help you run your life more efficiently and effectively. The goal is to develop an Absolute No list that, over time, makes you feel safe, protected, taken care of, and free to be your best self.

Resources

🌾 My book *Take Time for Your Life*—shows you how to take control of your outer world (including information on the Absolute Yes list) in order to create a peaceful inner world.

🌾 *The Portable Coach: 28 Surefire Strategies for Business and Personal Success,* by Thomas J. Leonard, with Byron Larson—offers you 28 ways to shape your life, career, and relationships so that they're satisfying and profitable.

🌾 *Body + Soul*—a magazine filled with great ideas on how to honor your priorities related to health, wellness, inner growth, and whole living. You can find more information at: **www.wholeliving.com**.

Chapter Seven

Soul-Loving Space

A re you in love with where you live? Do you feel energized and clearheaded at work? Before I became a coach (and started practicing Extreme Self-Care), my own home and office merely served as convenient and fairly comfortable roofs over my head. Then as I began to understand the concept of Extreme Self-Care, I slowly discovered that far beyond the point of functional was the experience of actually being *fed* by my environment. This meant creating soul-loving spaces that filled me with joy, gave me energy, inspired my best work (and thinking), and allowed me to express my creativity within a realm of peace and calm. Where I lived and worked both needed to reflect the things that were important to my soul.

In 2007, my husband and I moved into our dream house. For more than ten years we'd saved our money, pored over books and magazines for great ideas, visited home shows to learn about construction techniques, and envisioned what this dream house would look like. And while we were embarking on this journey, we lived in a beautiful, cottagelike abode where we both also worked.

During the last year, things were pretty tight and stressful. Michael and I shared a single closet in a small bedroom, and our living area was quickly filling up with furniture and materials for our new home. Although we loved our little place, after a while it had become cramped, cluttered, and draining. I felt the weight of this reality every single day. My life seemed constrained, my mind felt cluttered, and I just knew that I wouldn't be able to allow anything new into my life as long as we were there.

Finally, after years of searching for the right piece of land and working with an amazing architect and building team, we moved into our new home—a soul-nourishing place of beauty and light that includes the architectural elements my husband and I both adore from gothic cathedrals, medieval castles, and old-world classic designs. There's also an abundance of wildlife, beautiful views of nature from every window, and silence—something my nervous system craves.

Within a month of moving, I started to feel like a different person. I woke up with a smile on my face just about every day, regardless of what was going on in my life. As I moved through the rooms, I felt lighter, expansive, and rid of tension. I slept like a baby and often found myself humming during the day for no other reason than because I was in an environment that felt so good. Finally, our home had become a sanctuary . . . a sacred and holy place.

The True Impact of Our Surroundings

The power of being in a space that feels fully aligned with our soul is sorely underrated. In all my years of coaching (and in my own life), I've seen few ways to practice Extreme Self-Care that have a more dramatic, immediate effect on our quality of life than this one idea. I'm not just talking about clearing clutter or getting organized, although these are a huge part of the formula; I'm talking about recognizing the impact your home or office has on your emotional and physical health, your energy levels, your self-esteem, your relationship to yourself and others, and your spiritual well-being. It's called "creating a soul-nourishing environment," and I've seen this vital concept—the transformation of a person's home or office—literally transform his or her life.

A soul-loving environment is a home or office free from clutter and disorganization—a space filled with elements that allow us to be and act our best. When we live or work in a place that's crammed with too much stuff or devoid of beauty, it drains our energy. We end up feeling depressed, exhausted, and unmotivated. We don't function well, and this can ultimately end up affecting other areas of our lives. I've worked with many people, for example, who feel as if they're drowning in clutter and, over time, end up isolated because they're too embarrassed to share their home with others. I've also watched business owners struggle to bring in new clients while working in an outdated office that looks (and feels) like a black hole—not the best environment for courting new business.

Like a weed that wiggles its way through concrete to find the light, we adapt to our environment. If we tolerate a home that doesn't feel like us, chances are we'll tolerate a relationship that doesn't feel quite right either, or we'll stay working at a job that's just "okay." While the idea may seem a bit strange, experience has taught me that how we live "in here" at home translates into how we live "out there" in the world.

Your space says a lot about your life. To understand what I mean, take a look around your home or office and consider the following:

- 🍃 What do these surroundings say about you?

- 🍃 Do they reflect the essence of who you are?

- 🍃 If this space were to tell a story about your life, what story would it tell?

- 🍃 How does the space make you feel?

- 🍃 What have you been tolerating for too long?

- 🍃 What areas make you feel good? What areas make you feel bad? Why?

- 🍃 If you could sweep the whole room into the trash and start over, would you?

See what I mean? If you're like most people, chances are your home or office is less soul nourishing than you'd like. The most common reason for this has to do with the amount of stuff in our lives. So many of us become numb to the things that surround us. We end up living with cluttered countertops and desks, piles of unopened junk mail, or closets overflowing with clothes we rarely wear. Or we spend the majority of our waking hours in an office stacked with file folders, paperwork, or books. The sad truth is that a soulless home or office zaps our attention,

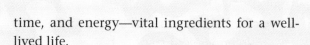

time, and energy—vital ingredients for a well-lived life.

Sometimes the most powerful way we can begin to create a soul-loving space is to simply remove 50 percent or more of what's there. I had a chance to experience this as soon as Michael and I moved into our new home. Prior to moving, we went through our belongings and gave away anything we no longer used or needed. Then, as an experiment, we made a decision to move only the bare necessities into our new house and put everything else into our garage so that we could experience what it felt like to live in the simplicity of space. What we learned surprised us.

As someone who has taught the principle of "When in doubt, throw it out" for years, I was amazed to discover that my husband and I still had way too much stuff. The decision to leave most of what we had in the garage so we could live in a state of "sacred simplicity" allowed us to experience what it felt like to be free of visual distractions—something we hadn't known for a long time. That decision taught me an important lesson.

When you're brave enough to let go of anything you don't absolutely love or need, what you have left is the space for stillness and possibility. And this state is quite appealing—so peaceful, calm, and relaxing that you naturally become very careful about what you let in. You raise your standards.

Michael and I indeed raised our standards, which led to our adopting a new rule: if it's not an absolute yes—something we really need or adore—then it won't come into our home. So instead of moving the remainder of our things from the garage inside, we decided to give most of it away. By doing so, we were able to share the wealth with others and create a home that feels spacious and elegant at the same time.

When you dedicate time and energy to creating a soul-nurturing environment, you give yourself an enormous gift. But don't take my word for it. Let's see what happens over the next month when you experience for yourself what it's like to fall in love with your home or office.

Extreme Self-Care Challenge: Create a Soul-Loving Space

During the next 30 days, I'd like you to focus on creating a soul-loving space in just one room that you spend a lot of time in, such as your bedroom, office, or kitchen. That way you can see and feel what it's like to love where you are. This process will serve as a motivating force for other spaces once you get the hang of the four-step process.

You don't need to build a new home to create a soul-nourishing space, and you certainly don't need to spend a lot of money. While there are wonderful books that detail smart strategies for getting organized and creating beautiful spaces, I'm going to keep this process simple by suggesting the following four steps:

1. Examine—consider how well this space measures up to a soul-nourishing environment.

2. Evaluate—determine what needs to change and how you need to change.

3. Eliminate—get rid of anything you don't absolutely love or need.

4. Enhance—make this space your version of "extraordinary" so that it reflects the essence of you.

Here we go. . . .

Step 1: Examine

Before you begin, I want you to examine what "soul nourishing" translates to in your chosen room. Consider these questions:

🌿 What does this room mean to you?

🌿 What's the primary purpose of this room?

🌿 What must you have here in order to honor your soul?

🌿 What must you not have?

As you consider these questions, you might determine that the primary purpose of your sunroom, for example, is to rejuvenate and replenish your spirit after a long day. You realize that in order for this room to be a soul-nourishing space, it needs to be quiet and serene and have clear, clean energy.

Step 2: Evaluate

The next step is to conduct an honest assessment of the room to see what specifically needs to be changed in order to make it a soul-nourishing environment. Set aside an hour for this step.

With a notepad and pen in hand, simply write down what you'd like to see done to this room. As you walk around the room, use the following questions as your guide:

🌿 Starting with a simple one-to-ten scale, with one being that you loathe this space and ten being that you love it, how would you rate the overall room?

When you think about what needs to change, what immediately comes to mind?

 What items are important to you?

 What things could you easily let go of?

 What needs to be added to make this room more soulful?

 What are some of your favorite elements here? Do you love the lighting, a view from a window, or the height of the ceilings?

 When you think about what this room represents, how will making this space more soul nourishing affect other areas of your life? For example, if you're single and you choose to work on your bedroom, it may improve your chances of attracting a wonderful new mate.

 What do you need to do to be sure that this space remains clutter free and soulful?

Let's look at an example. Imagine that you've decided to work on your bedroom, and when you examine the space you notice that you love the light and the spaciousness of the room, but it feels cluttered. Then when you evaluate the changes that need to be made, you notice that you have a pile of magazines and books next to your bed that drain your energy. You also have a nightstand with too much stuff on it, a closet that's full, and piles of paperwork on the floor that make it difficult to navigate around in the dark.

Every night as you get ready to go to sleep, you feel frustrated when you have to maneuver around the obstacles or when you knock something off the nightstand. When you evaluate this area using the one-to-ten scale, you note your dissatisfaction level is at a two (which might come as a surprise, especially if you've gotten really good at blocking out your environment).

When you think about the cost of keeping the room this way, you realize that this mess interferes with your ability to get a good night's sleep. And by clearing this space, you know that you'll not only feel more relaxed, but there's also a good chance that you might even be tempted to get to bed earlier (something you've been meaning to do).

Got the idea? Finally, before you move to the next step—eliminate—you'll want to make note of what you'll need in order to prepare for it. When you look at your bedroom, for instance, you may realize that you'll require a new home for your favorite books in this space because keeping them next to your bed feels like a call to action rather than rest. Next, you'll want to find a place to donate the volumes that you no longer want to keep. Then you'll need shelves for those you move to another area of your home. And finally, you'll want to plan to donate your old magazines to the gym, a nursing home, or a nearby hospital.

Step 3: Eliminate

The third step in creating a soul-nurturing environment is the elimination stage. Here, you'll be focused on eliminating two things: (1) the habits and behaviors that have created a less-than-desirable home or office, and (2) anything you don't absolutely love or need.

First up are the habits. Consider this:

- ❧ What do you do to contribute to making this a less-than-desirable space?

- ❧ Are you a guaranteed repository for other people's giveaways?

- ❧ Do you let the mail pile up?

- ❧ Do you hoard paper and information, insisting that you might need it someday?

- ❧ Do you deprive yourself of the tools you need to stay organized, such as a

filing cabinet or a closet system that will allow you to tame your unruly clothes?

It's important to look at the *source* of your space problem *before* you start cleaning house (or office), otherwise you'll wind up right back in the same dilemma in a few short months (or weeks!). So if you have a habit of throwing your worn clothes on the back of a chair in your bedroom, either train yourself to hang them up right away or buy yourself a big laundry basket and put them in there and out of sight. Trace the problem to its source. If you can't hang your clothes up because there's no room in your closet, then you'll not only want to get rid of some clothes, you might even need to put a moratorium on shopping until you're able to limit what you buy.

Once you have a handle on the habits that need to be changed, it's time to start clearing your space. To keep it simple, make four piles:

— **Pile #1: Things you'll give away to loved ones.** These are the items you feel sentimental about or that hold special meaning but need to go because you don't absolutely love them anymore. The value of giving away once-treasured items to those you love is twofold. First, it's easier to pass on something meaningful to someone who will appreciate its value. It can actually motivate you to let go of more than you normally would. Second, there's a good chance that you'll

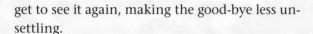

get to see it again, making the good-bye less unsettling.

— Pile #2: Things you'll give away to strangers. Remember to do your homework in the evaluation stage so that you have a plan about where things will go. When you share your wealth with those in need, it can provide a powerful motivating force for letting go of more than you think you can. Look for (and visit) a local shelter or crisis center to get a good idea of the work they do in service to others. This is a great trip to make with children, too, so the whole family gets on board and your children have a firsthand experience of what it's like to share their things with those in need. Trust me, once you have an emotional connection to a place, you'll find the inspiration to let go of even more stuff.

— Pile #3: Things that can be recycled. Check with your local recycling center for a list of items that can be reused. You'll be surprised at how much can be recycled or put to good use elsewhere.

— Pile #4: Things that simply need to be thrown away. Before you get started on this pile, make sure that you've found a place where you'll be able to throw these things out. Is there a junk-removal service in your area or a shredding truck that can come to your home to dispose of outdated financial records? Could you share the cost with a buddy, or with members of your Life Makeover Group who are doing this work with you? Do you know the hours of your local dump or when you can put certain items out in the trash? Remember that preplanning provides the motivation you'll need to follow through.

Step 4: Enhance

The final stage of creating a soul-loving home or office is the best part of all. It has to do with enhancement, and the name of the game is beauty—a universal need that feeds our soul.

What does beauty mean to you? What inspires you to fall in love with your home or office? For some people it's clear, wide-open space and sunlight. For others it's creative inspiration in the form of artwork, photos of loved ones and favorite life experiences, or brightly colored walls. Some find beauty in the tools that allow them to feel organized and able to do their best work, such as a broad-topped desk or big-screen monitor. The enhancements you make to your home or office may be practical in nature, but they also need to serve the number one priority of adding beauty to the environment.

When you begin to add things to your space, let *your* version of beauty be the guide. Go through magazines, catalogs, and decorating books; or browse through stores looking for the shapes, colors, and textures that catch your eye and hold your interest. I've personally found great inspiration at museums, in movies, and in beautiful old hotels.

Raise your standards. For example, if you need shelves in your office to hold supplies, you might consider buying a beautiful armoire with elegantly carved wood doors rather than a wall of plain or open shelves. If you have a window in your kitchen that looks out over a neighbor's porch, you could get creative and cover it with flowering plants or a bird feeder.

Don't let financial constraints prevent you from believing that you can add beauty to your space. Some of my best purchases have cost very little. I love searching for treasures in secondhand shops and flea markets. The items found there may require a bit of enhancement themselves, such as some paint or a minor repair, but see it as another opportunity for you to add your own unique sense of style and beauty to the room.

If you're unsure of how to add beauty to your space, ask for help from someone who has a home or office you admire, or from a professional decorator or designer. Just make sure it's *your* sense of style and not theirs that's dictating the choices.

Once you've finished creating a soul-loving space in one room this month, bask in the feeling of joy and contentment while in this space. Then use those feelings to fuel work on the next room!

Resources

🌿 *Interior Divine: Walking You Through the Transformation of Your Home,* by Jayne M. Pelosi— helps you become acquainted with your own design personality.

🌿 *Sacred Space: Clearing and Enhancing the Energy of Your Home,* by Denise Linn—offers a spiritual approach to space enhancement and shows you how to dramatically transform your life by changing the environment in your home or office. I've used Denise's suggestions and have had amazing results.

🌿 Got Books? (**www.gotbooks.com**)—an organization dedicated to finding good homes for used books. While they are based in New England, anyone can send them donations. (You may also want to try your local library for ideas on where to donate books in your community.)

- *It's All Too Much: An Easy Plan for Living a Richer Life with Less Stuff,* by Peter Walsh—a great guide for clutter management.

- *Buried in Treasures: Help for Compulsive Acquiring, Saving, and Hoarding,* by David F. Tolin, Randy O. Frost, and Gail Steketee—a program for helping compulsive hoarders dig their way out of the clutter and chaos of their homes or offices.

- *Organizing from the Inside Out: The Foolproof System for Organizing Your Home, Your Office, and Your Life (Second Edition),* by Julie Morgenstern—great advice from a top organizational consultant.

- *O at Home*—a beautiful magazine filled with great ways to enhance your environment.

Chapter Eight

You're So Sensitive

When I was a little girl, my dad used to call me "Sarah Heartburn"—a funny twist on the name of French movie actress Sarah Bernhardt—because I had a tendency to be a bit dramatic when things didn't go my way. The truth was that I was a highly sensitive child. I cried easily, felt deeply hurt when kids called me names or made fun of me, and was prone to bouts of loneliness and a kind of sadness that I didn't understand. It wasn't until I read *The Highly Sensitive Person,* by Elaine Aron as an adult that I figured out what was going on. It was one of those rare experiences when a book seems to put your whole life into perspective and you suddenly understand yourself in a brand-new way.

For years I used to beat myself up for being sensitive. Like the little girl who felt too much, as a grown woman I still cried easily, felt bowled over by too much stimulation (the kind that came from big crowds, bright lights, and loud noises), and was deeply hurt by criticism and mean-spirited remarks. I hated being sensitive—loathed it, in fact—until a conversation with Thomas Leonard shifted my perspective.

I had delivered one of my first speeches on coaching and had received criticism from an angry audience member who didn't like the way I presented my ideas. The review was harsh, and the pain of it stayed with me for days. During a call to Thomas, I described the feedback and admitted, "I hate that I'm so affected by this stuff. You can't believe what's gone on in my head since I read that review: *I suck as a speaker; Forget about doing this for a living; Stick to being a coach, kid.* I'm just too sensitive, and I hate it!"

Thomas listened thoughtfully as I continued on about how upset I was, and when I finished, he delivered one of his classic one-liners: "You know, Cheryl, the way I see it, your sensitivity is your greatest gift." After taking a moment to allow his statement to sink in, he continued, "This gift has gotten you to where you are today, and it's what makes you a great coach. If I were you, I'd protect your sensitivity rather than hate it."

Protect my sensitivity? Now there was a concept I'd never considered before. The idea that my sensitivity might be a blessing rather than a curse was a surprising revelation. Like so many men and women, I believed that being vulnerable and expressing it was akin to admitting defeat or appearing weak. For example, it wasn't okay to get emotional about a boss's inappropriate behavior; I needed to suck it up and get the job done anyway. Now Thomas was challenging me to reconsider those beliefs.

As I thought about the benefits of my sensitivity, I realized that it had always led me to feel deeply connected to nature, animals, birds, music, and art. It had also translated into a keenly perceptive ability to read people. With a tilt of the head, a blink of an eye, or a slight shift in tone of voice, I often could tell what someone was thinking or feeling. This ability developed over time into a finely tuned intuitive knowing that allowed me to be quite effective as a coach and teacher. I could anticipate people's needs. Many times I knew what my students wanted before they knew themselves. As I listened carefully to a client who was trying to find his or her way, I could see a path form that showed us both which direction to go in. And I often found myself choosing—with my heart, not my head—the exact words someone needed to hear.

I began to understand that there are all kinds of gifts we experience when we open to, and then embrace, our sensitive side. All human beings possess a level of sensitivity that, when taken seriously and protected, can open us up to a rich and satisfying experience of life. When we give presence to our sensitivity, we're better able to see beauty everywhere and in everything from flowers to weeds, in joyous experiences and in the poignantly sad ones as well. We tend to be empathetic—kind and compassionate people who can easily put ourselves in the shoes of another. These are wonderful gifts indeed.

How to Protect Your Own Sensitivity

My decision to protect my sensitivity was one of the most influential acts of Extreme Self-Care I've ever taken in my life. It forced me to stop judging and disowning essential parts of myself and start honoring who I am at my core. It's funny, but once I made a decision to embrace my sensitivity, it did the opposite of what I expected. Rather than leave me feeling like a pincushion in a world full of pins, it actually made me stronger and better able to use my gifts.

Instead of using my energy to keep my feelings under wraps, I learned to take steps to create the safety necessary to express them freely. For example, while writing this book, I carefully chose the people who would read the first draft. In order to write from a heartfelt, vulnerable place—the best one to connect with readers—I needed to make sure that members of the team would be respectful with their feedback. So, once I was ready to pass the book along, I let everyone know the kind of critique I wanted and the way I needed it to be delivered. By protecting my sensitivity, I could write from an authentic place.

So how do you begin to protect your own sensitivity? By becoming aware of the people, places, and things that cause you to shut down, numb out, or leave the present moment. Sensitivity is about being open and receptive to life. It's about being in the present moment, right here, right now, with your soul's antenna fully engaged so that you can tune in to the magic and beauty life has to offer.

Let's take a look at some examples of how you might protect your sensitivity. As you read through them, underline the suggestions and ideas that appeal to you.

1. Step into the Moment

Presence ignites sensitivity. When we're ruminating about the past or worrying about the future, we miss the only real experience we can ever have: the one that's happening right now in this moment. It's in the present that we find the richness and meaning we long for. One of the first things we need to do to protect our sensitivity is pull our attention back to the now. This is the place where we feel truly alive.

To practice bringing yourself into the present moment, you need to get in the habit of managing your mind. You can do this in simple ways every day. When driving in the car, feel your hands on the wheel and your foot on the gas, and notice the scenery passing by. When talking on the phone, actually feel it in your hand, notice the depth of your breathing, or take note of how you're sitting or standing. Tuning in to the sensations in your body—the energy that enlivens it—will automatically bring you back to the here-and-now.

2. Turn Down the Noise

Sensitivity is nurtured by silence. When you stop and listen to your life, you'll probably notice that you're surrounded by noise all the time. For example, close your eyes and tune in to your environment right now. What's plugged in, turned on, and making noise? Is there a computer humming or a television running in the background, or is someone in another part of the house making racket? Are there phones ringing, people talking, or copy machines whirring in your office? Maybe you live in a busy city where whistles, sirens, and construction sounds are par for the course. Whatever the case, it's important to know that such disturbances affect your mind and body. When there's too much noise in your environment, you naturally have to shut down some part of your senses just to manage the auditory stress.

There are many benefits to turning down the noise in your life. When you have peace and quiet, you'll feel clearheaded and relaxed. Your body (and your nervous system) will shift to a healthier, more balanced state that allows the fight-or-flight system to rest. And you'll have more energy. After all, your body absorbs and processes every sound, whether you realize it or not, and processing sound takes energy. That's why many people feel exhausted after spending time in crowds at a party or while shopping at a busy mall.

I thrive in silence. I rarely have ringers turned on in my home, I mute commercials while watching TV (although digital recording is quickly making this habit a thing of the past), and I love to work in an office where there's an absolute hush. For me, the less noise the better. When I'm writing, I know that a still space gives me much better access to creativity, wisdom, and insight; as well as the ability to solve problems with ease. Answers to the questions I might previously have struggled with often emerge from the quiet.

To get an idea of how turning down the noise can benefit you, start with small steps. Instead of starting the washing machine first thing in the morning, enjoy a quiet house for a while once the kids have left for school. Try arriving at work early before everyone else does, so you can see what it's like to work in a more peaceful setting. While driving to the office, turn the radio off now and then and commute in silence. Stop falling asleep to the sound of the TV when you go to bed at night.

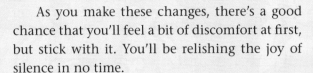
As you make these changes, there's a good chance that you'll feel a bit of discomfort at first, but stick with it. You'll be relishing the joy of silence in no time.

3. Stop the Violence

Another way to protect your sensitivity is to limit your exposure to all forms of sensational or violent news. The level of terror and anxiety contained in most media stories is toxic to the nervous system, and it's getting worse all the time. Television "teasers" are almost always fear based. You know the ones: "Tune in at 11 to see what dangers might be lurking in your drinking water!" or "Don't miss the 5 o'clock news to find out if a sexual predator is living in your neighborhood right now!" The news is frightening, negative, and often shallow—and when you take it in on a regular basis, you have no choice but to shut down to handle the emotional stress.

Anything that desensitizes you to some aspect of life sets you up to tolerate less than what you deserve. If you have to repeatedly numb yourself to handle the news, for instance, this numb state gets carried over into your life at large and may make it easier to ignore a snide remark from a co-worker. Being shut down can also cause you to miss important signals. For example, you might tune out your child's constant complaining about how much she hates school

and neglect to see that she's in real trouble and needs some kind of intervention.

I rarely watch the news, and I immediately recycle any piece of marketing material that uses fear to relay its message. Instead, I use the Internet to choose how I'll stay informed. My browser's home page is customized to only cover the Websites that are most important to me, and if one of my favorite sources starts down the path of fear-based headlines, I remove it. I love talk radio and am pleased to see the increase in personal-growth-related shows. I tune in to HayHouseRadio.com, National Public Radio, or Oprah & Friends on XM Satellite Radio.

As you start paying closer attention to what you expose your eyes and ears to, ask yourself, "Does this encourage or discourage my sensitivity?" Then choose accordingly.

4. Put Limits on Toxic People

Are there individuals in your life who consistently dump their frustration, anger, disappointment, old emotional wounds, or unfinished business on you without doing anything to change their behavior? You know, the men and women who make you anxious when you're around them—the ones who require you to put up some kind of a guard? The need to shield yourself from them is a signal that you're entering an "unsafe sensitivity zone." Anyone who consistently puts you down, chronically complains about how miserable they are without doing anything about it, criticizes you, or sucks your energy is affecting your ability to remain openhearted and sensitive. In fact, it's dangerous to be open and receptive in such a toxic environment.

We all have unhealed places, and there's a good chance that at one time or another, each one of us fits neatly into the category of being a threat to someone else's sensitivity. That's called being "a human in the evolutionary process." No, what I'm referring to here are the men and women who refuse to take responsibility for their actions—the ones who hurt for sport, make a career out of complaining, or who get off on putting other people down. If there are people like that in your life, you'll need to protect your sensitivity by setting limits. You'll either need to have an honest conversation about how things need to change, limit the time you spend in their company, or avoid them altogether. Be it family, friends, co-workers, a boss, or a neighbor, *no one* has the right to rob you of your sensitivity.

5. Manage Technology

In this day and age of "let me get to you whenever I want or need to," we have to be more vigilant than ever about how and when we use technology to protect our sensitivity. Between cell phones, text messaging, and e-mail, most of us are plugged in and available 24/7. And the ease with which we can be in touch will only increase as technology becomes more personal and accessible. So we need to remember who's in charge— the trick is to manage technology in such a way that we become *responders,* not reactors.

As I said earlier, I rarely have the telephone ringers turned on in my home or office. When I have in the past, I've acted like one of Pavlov's dogs, quickly jumping to attention at the sound of the bell. A ringing phone, chiming text, or beeping e-mail alert is a call to action for most humans. When an alarm of some sort gets triggered, not only does our brain say, "Hey, there's something to do!" this unplanned interruption also activates our body's fight-or-flight response. Ready and on alert, it becomes difficult to relax when we're waiting for the next interruption. So rather than have that happen to me, I now let phone calls go to voice mail so that I can choose to handle them at my convenience.

Another important way to manage technology is to carefully plan how and when you'll respond to voice mail, e-mails, or text messages. The length of time it takes for you to return a message gives those around you a clear indication as to how available you are. If someone sends an e-mail with a question, for instance, and you respond immediately, you essentially teach that person to expect an immediate response in the future. This can get tricky if you get a lot of phone calls or e-mails—and many of us do.

While your job may require a quick turn-around, make it a point to look for other ways to extend that time whenever possible (or to eliminate the need to respond at all). Let friends and family know that it might take a week to return messages rather than 24 hours. Take more time before you respond to nonurgent work e-mails. Also, look for ways to cut back on e-mail altogether. If you're someone who gets hundreds of messages a day (a sad but true reality in today's workforce), put a process in place that dramatically reduces this drag on your energy. Get together with co-workers and talk about strategies to reduce the number of e-mails sent throughout the office. Trust me, this productive conversation should be a priority in any busy company. Let people off the hook so that they no longer feel the need to cover themselves by copying you on their exchanges. Or get in the habit of filing the messages that you need to keep as soon as you've read them so they don't pile up in your in-box.

Don't get caught up in the false belief that if you scramble to respond to everyone, you'll free up your time to finally relax. While this works for some individuals, experience has taught me that they are few and far between. Think about it . . . when's the last time you were caught up on *every* message and felt free?

6. Set the Mood

Knowing the kind of environment that suits you best is another way to care for your sensitive side. Take my best friend, Max, who's a stickler for good lighting. She hates bright lights, so she's become masterful at using lamps to create a relaxed, peaceful mood in any room. And my colleague Martin always knows the right restaurant to choose when gathering a small group of friends or clients together. Not only does he make sure the lighting is right, but he also ensures that the noise level is conducive to easy conversation.

As for you, maybe you'd like to create a more harmonious work environment by using a warmly lit desk lamp instead of glaring overhead fluorescent bulbs. Again, keep in mind how important the little details can be for your Extreme Self-Care.

❧

There are so many ways to protect your sensitivity. Maybe you've decided to forgo the frenetic energy of shopping malls by buying what you need online. Perhaps you've chosen clothing, sheets, or towels that are so soft they feel wonderful next to your sensitive skin. Or you may have decided to hold smaller dinner parties so that you have the time you need to visit more intimately with friends—that way, you can avoid the overstimulation that comes with larger groups.

Before we get to this month's challenge, I want to make one final point about sensitivity and children. Years ago I had an encounter with a mother that touched me in a memorable way. This woman stood in line for more than an hour after one of my talks just to tell me how important it was for her to hear about the concept of sensitivity as a gift that needed to be honored and protected. "All this time I thought I was doing my son a favor by trying to toughen him up," she confessed. "Instead of nurturing his gentler, creative side, I've been pushing him to find a career that will pay well and allow him to live a good, productive life. I can see now that I'm making a mistake. He's a talented young artist, and while I need to teach him responsibility, I also need to encourage his sensitive side."

I couldn't agree more. Start early and teach your children about the importance of protecting their sensitivity. Trust me, it's the gift that delivers a rich and meaningful life.

Extreme Self-Care Challenge: Protect Your Sensitivity

This month's challenge is all about protecting your sensitivity. To get started, you'll want to use your notebook or journal to do a little research. First, I want you to go back through this chapter and make a list of all of the examples you chose to underline. Next, use the following questions to help you identify five specific ways that you'll start protecting your sensitivity this month:

1. Where do you need to turn down the noise in your environment?

2. How will you limit the violent and disturbing news that comes into your life on a daily basis?

3. Who in your life zaps your energy, causes you anxiety, or makes you feel on guard? How will you protect yourself from this person?

4. What changes do you need to make to better manage technology so that you can respond to the needs of others rather than react?

5. Taking into account your five senses, what kind of surroundings do you need to feel relaxed and present?

Write down one action step for each question and implement it within the next 30 days. At the end of each week, take some time to write about the positive ways these steps have changed your life.

Resources

⚜ Daryn Kagan's Website (**www.darynkagan.com**)—a great site dedicated to providing good news, inspirational stories, and hope by showing what's possible.

⚜ *The Highly Sensitive Person: How to Thrive When the World Overwhelms You,* by Elaine N. Aron, Ph.D.—a wonderful resource for understanding and working with sensitivity.

⚜ *The Highly Sensitive Child: Helping Our Children Thrive When the World Overwhelms Them,* by Elaine N. Aron, Ph.D.—covers raising sensitive children.

⚜ Elaine Aron's Website (**www.hsperson.com**)—contains self-tests and excellent information for the highly sensitive person.

⚜ *The Highly Sensitive Person's Survival Guide: Essential Skills for Living Well in an Overstimulating World,* by Ted Zeff, Ph.D.—a step-by-step guide that will enable you to thrive as a highly sensitive person.

Chapter Nine

Tune-up Time

The foundation of a good life is good health. While the concept of Extreme Self-Care can be applied to all areas of your life—career, spiritual well-being, relationships, and so on—what supports each of these areas is the care you provide for the amazing vehicle that takes you through life.

Over the last two years as I've dealt with Michael's illness, I've witnessed firsthand what happens to a family when one member is faced with a health crisis. Life as you know it comes to a halt. Roles get switched, strain gets put on a marriage, financial pressure sets in, and your whole world suddenly revolves around getting your loved one well. There's nothing like such a crisis to drive home the message most of us have heard at one time or another: "Without your health, you have nothing." Caring for your body is one of the most important investments of time and energy you can make.

This month's focus is on Extreme Self-Care and the body, but not on the areas that you typically see written about—diet, exercise, and losing weight. Instead, we'll focus on the actions you can take to make sure your body is in the best shape it can be in *right now*.

Take Stock of Your Health

When we get busy or overwhelmed, it's far too easy to take our body for granted. In the last few years, I've heard from more and more people who put off making (and keeping) appointments that are directly related to their health and physical well-being. It's not until we're faced with a problem that we understand the value of maintaining and caring for our body *before* a problem arises.

There are a variety of reasons why we don't get the care we deserve. For many, the challenge has to do with money and the lack of health insurance, which is a big issue for millions of people here in the United States. I remember very clearly what it was like not to be able to afford health coverage when I first started my business and was living alone. For years I put off whatever appointments I could, until one day I got very sick and realized that the care of my body was a far more important investment than the clothes, books, or socializing that had been on my list of expenditures. My body needed to move up to the top of that list.

Once I made the decision to make my health a priority, I went to town researching options for someone in my position: a woman with limited income, living alone, and getting by paycheck to paycheck. I found a program through the state of Massachusetts that provided low-cost medical care to those in need, depending on income. I relied on this program to provide me with coverage for two years, until I could afford to pay for insurance on my own. Then I was able to buy a policy that provided catastrophic coverage—a low-cost option that covered me for accidents or emergency services. Eventually I came to afford a higher level of insurance as my earnings increased.

The point of the story is that your health is a priority that matters. Whether you barter your skills for the services of others, such as a massage, facials, or a haircut (something I did for years); negotiate lower costs with medical providers as an uninsured patient (something I also did); find a financial-assistance program in your community (don't assume there isn't one); or give up spending in one area to allow for the health-care appointments you need, caring for your body is one of the best investments you'll ever make.

For many of us, the decision to put off making health appointments also has to do with fear . . . the fear of finding out that something is wrong. Now more than ever, because of the enormous amount of media coverage and marketing material focused on illness, we've become hypersensitive to symptoms and disease. As a result, we suffer in silence, afraid that we might have some kind of serious problem. So we often avoid doctors altogether.

Think of your body as a classic automobile—a beautiful Rolls-Royce—and stop for a moment to consider the care this amazing vehicle might need. It's probably high time for a tune-up, so take the opportunity to check out the different parts of your body that may need your attention.

Begin by answering the following questions:

1. Is there a health-related issue that you're concerned about? Several clients I've worked with in the past have waited months (and sometimes years!) to have a suspicious lump or mole checked, out of a concern that it might be bad news. Although you may be under the false assumption that ignoring the problem gives you peace of mind, the truth is that your fear—conscious or not—is always running in the background. Like a virus or spyware program hidden on your computer, fear takes energy and resources, whether you realize it or not. If you don't believe me, think about a time when you finally did something you'd avoided for a while, such as going to the dentist or getting a mammogram. Then remember the palpable sense of relief you felt once the appointment was done and you knew everything was all right.

2. Is there something about your physical appearance that you feel self-conscious about? Do your teeth need to be straightened, or are your feet so sore that you're limited to one pair of shoes? Maybe your hair is thinning or you feel uncomfortable about your posture. These kinds of concerns can have quite an impact on the quality of your life when addressed.

I remember working with a woman who was so self-conscious about her crooked teeth (and so afraid of the dentist) that she never smiled. That's right, she worked hard to make sure that she *didn't* show her teeth. Now imagine the effect not smiling had on her disposition and mood, let alone the quality of her entire life. It's no wonder that once this woman had her teeth repaired, she felt like a completely different person. Life began to smile upon her, and suddenly she was meeting new people, having fun with friends, and laughing in a way she hadn't in years. Her willingness to face her fear and make her dental health a priority gave her a brand-new life.

3. Are you overdue for a routine maintenance appointment? Review the list below and see if there are certain self-care items that need your attention. As you read over the list, notice which items spark an "I've been meaning to get to that one" response:

🪷 Have you had a complete physical in the last year?

🪷 When was the last time you had an eye exam?

🪷 Is a trip to the dentist in order?

🪷 How's your back? Have you been intending to see a chiropractor or make an appointment with a massage therapist?

🪷 Are you happy with your hair, or do you need to see a professional stylist to get a fresh cut or color?

🪷 Have you had a manicure or a pedicure lately? (Yes, I'm talking to you guys, too.) If it sounds like an indulgence, stop to consider how much work your hands and feet do to support you!

🪷 How about a facial? Although this might seem like a luxury, trust me—as you get older, you'll be glad that you've taken good care of your skin.

🪷 Is it time for a mammogram or prostate screening?

These are just some examples of the basic body-care areas that, when handled, go a long way in supporting your emotional and physical self-care.

Get the Care You Deserve

Once you decide to overcome your procrastination or face your fear and get the tune-up you deserve, here are some important Extreme Self-Care guidelines that will support you:

1. Take Charge of Your Health

The first thing you need to know when practicing Extreme Self-Care as it pertains to the body is that you have to take full responsibility for your health. No more relying solely on doctors and other health-care professionals to tell you what to do. This means getting educated about your body: listening to health programs online or on the radio; reading books that teach you about how your body works; exploring complementary or holistic treatment options in addition to traditional modalities; or learning about nutrition, exercise, healthy cooking, or ways to make your body stronger. (I've included some of my favorite programs and Websites in the resource section at the end of this chapter.)

Over the years I've become quite an avid health enthusiast. I love learning about new ways to care for my body, mind, and spirit. I've come a long way from the young woman who feasted on fast food and sweets and only exercised when she wanted to lose weight—now I'm someone who buys organic fruits and vegetables, works out every day, loves learning about medical breakthroughs and advances, and has written extensively about the link between lifestyle choices and longevity.

Becoming an educated and experienced patient takes time and commitment, but it's worth the investment. When a health issue arises (and chances are it will), you'll feel much more empowered and able to make smart choices if you're a well-informed partner in your health.

2. Listen to Your Body

So many of us live from the neck up, so overwhelmed by all there is to do that, as a result, we end up missing important signals from our body that provide us with valuable information.

How well do you respond to the needs of your own body? Do you eat when you're hungry, sleep when you're tired, or take a break before you start to feel stressed? Learning to pay attention to such signals will go a long way in keeping you informed about what you need to do to keep your body in shape. Overlooking these signals, on the other hand, can cause trouble. For example, disregarding back pain can lead to the day when you make one little move and your back gives out altogether. Or ignoring your hunger pangs can lead to feeling so famished that you make a mad dash for the vending machine and end up eating candy for lunch.

Learning to connect your head with your body provides you with information that will not only allow you to protect your physical health, but will also lead you to make better choices that honor your emotional and spiritual wellness. When you stop to check in with your body before responding to a request, chances are you'll make the optimal decision. And as you learn to pay attention to the signals that your body gives you every day, you'll find that it becomes a wise and trustworthy partner.

Try it now by noticing how your body feels, at this very moment, as you answer the following questions:

❧ Are you hungry? If so, what does your body really need to feel nourished?

❧ Are you tired? Have you had enough sleep?

❧ Do you need to go to the bathroom? (You'd be amazed at how many people ignore this important signal.)

❧ Is there tension, discomfort, or stress anywhere? Mentally scan your body from head to toe.

❧ What part of your body feels weak or tired?

❧ What part of it feels strong?

❧ Do you notice any emotions connected to your body? For example, do you feel a sense of dread in the pit of your stomach about a meeting you need to attend, or a sense of warmth and excitement in your heart at the memory of a recent encounter with a loved one?

The more you practice tuning in to your body, the more you'll respond to its needs in a wise and intelligent way. Remember that when you pay attention to the sensations you feel, you shift your awareness to the present moment—the wisest place to live. Then as you notice what your body needs, you'll begin to respond quickly and effectively. Your feelings will become powerful messengers that direct your actions toward healing. You'll tolerate less stress because you'll catch the symptoms sooner and take action to alleviate the source. This helps prevent illness later on.

3. Choose Health Partners, Not Parents

The old days of giving your power away to health-care professionals are over. As someone who now practices Extreme Self-Care, it's imperative that you find health- and body-care providers who treat you like an equal, mature partner involved in his or her health. Anyone who touches your body—a doctor, dentist, nurse-practitioner, massage therapist, or hairstylist—should be someone you trust and feel supported by. This means that you'll need to do your homework to find the best fit.

Interview a variety of health-care providers to create a great team of professionals who will aid you in taking good care of your body. When searching for these providers, the goal is to find a *partner,* someone who will back your commitment to be responsible for your overall health and well-being, not an authority figure who tells you what to do. This person should have a good bedside manner and the ability to address all of your questions and concerns in a professional, easy-to-understand way, especially the questions that you're most afraid to discuss.

To find the type of health-care providers who will serve you best, start by asking your most discerning friends and family members for recommendations. Next, check with nurses—they're a wonderful source for medical information and referrals. Chances are there's someone in your life who knows a nurse.

Along with the normal ones about background, experience, and education, here are some questions you might ask when interviewing partners:

🌸 What's your basic philosophy when it comes to health?

🌸 Can you describe your ideal client/patient?

🌸 How available are you to your clients/patients? What's the best way to communicate with you?

🌸 How long do you intend to be with this practice?

In addition to asking these questions, be sure to pay attention to the quality of your experience when you do see someone. Ask yourself:

🌸 How did I feel about the office environment?

🌸 Was the staff friendly and pleasant enough for my taste?

🌸 Did I have to wait longer than I would have liked? Was I informed of the wait ahead of time?

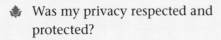

🍂 Was my privacy respected and protected?

🍂 Did I feel comfortable asking questions?

🍂 Did I feel relaxed or rushed?

🍂 Do I receive return phone calls within a time frame that feels comfortable to me?

Like the feeling you have after a great first date, you should leave an office feeling good about your encounter with any professional.

Next, once you've found the right doctor, dentist, hairstylist, or aesthetician, you need to become a responsible partner—someone who recognizes that it's ultimately your responsibility to take care of your body. This means planning questions ahead of time, inquiring about all of your options, knowing the products or equipment that will be used on your body, and being clear about your needs so that you can convey them directly.

4. Find the Right Emotional Support

At some point in your life, there's a good chance that a health concern (or the need for an appointment) will arise that will make you feel anxious or nervous. This is when having support—the right support—makes all the difference in the world. Knowing whom you can turn to when you need a calming presence during a health crisis is essential in practicing Extreme Self-Care.

My colleague Pam knows that if she requires a medical test that may cause her pain, her partner is *not* the person to bring along. It only took one experience for the two of them to find out that there had better be a couch around to catch him when he falls. On the other hand, my husband is a knowledgeable health professional and someone who can provide solid emotional support, so he's my first choice for comfort and guidance whenever I'm faced with a health concern.

When you get sick and need someone to turn to, you want to choose a person who rates low on the drama scale, someone you won't have to take care of when the going gets tough. As a matter of fact, sometimes doing what's best for you means *not* telling others about what's going on until you have all of the information and details you need. If you know that your sister will freak out about the lump found on your mammogram, for instance, chances are she's not the woman to contact once you get the news that you need further testing. Calling your best friend or your therapist might be a better choice. And if your partner or spouse gets frantic when you're sick, you may need to have a good friend spend the night when you get home from surgery just to make sure that you can rest easy during the recovery period.

There are a variety of ways to get the support you deserve when feeling anxious about health issues. You might ask a family member to help you find a sensitive dentist and then accompany you to the appointment. (If you have a fear of dentists, you're not alone. It's always been the number one fear of my clients as well.) Or you could ask a friend to do some Web research on a particular illness or disease so that you're not overwhelmed or frightened by what you see.

5. Know What You Need to Know, When You Need to Know It

Whenever I have any test done on my body—a mammogram, an ultrasound, an allergy test, some blood work, or what have you—I always do the following:

❧ I find out exactly how long it will take to get the results, as well as exactly how and when I'll be notified.

❧ I ask to have a copy of the results faxed directly to my home office at the same time they're sent to my doctor. (We all have a right to have access to our own medical records.)

❧ I follow up immediately as soon as the results are scheduled to be in.

Over the years I've become quite knowledgeable about reading and understanding medical test results. Because I've taken an active role in my health care, and because I like to know what's going on with my body, I make it a point of working with doctors and nurse-practitioners who freely share information. Receiving test results directly may not be for everyone, however. You need to know what's right for you. Sometimes it's better to let your doctor receive and digest the results before discussing them with you. The point is to know what *you* need to know to feel safe and supported, when you need to know it.

Modern medicine has reached an unprecedented ability to treat and cure a multitude of health problems, so start feeling empowered about your health. Your body is an amazing vehicle that takes you through this journey called life. Regular checkups, early detection, and nurturing appointments that care for it are all part of taking good care of you.

Extreme Self-Care Challenge: Care for Your Body

This month's Extreme Self-Care challenge is all about caring for your body. It's time to listen to what it needs so you can schedule those health appointments that might be overdue. So I'd like you to do two things for the next 30 days:

— Practice **tuning in to your body** by stopping periodically and noticing how you feel. Does your neck feel tight? Do you need to go to the bathroom? Are you hungry? Are you making decisions that feel right in your gut? To help keep you focused, I want you to make two signs that each say CHECK IN WITH YOUR BODY. Hang one on the bathroom mirror, and put the other in a place where you'll see it throughout the day— maybe taped to your cell phone or hanging in your office. Then each morning as you brush your teeth, take a few moments to conduct a body scan. Mentally go down, from the top of your head to the tips of your toes, and simply notice what you feel. Pay attention to any places that hold tension, tightness, or discomfort of any sort. Throughout the day, continue to check in by asking your body what it needs.

— Because caring for your health is an ongoing process, it's helpful to **make a plan of action** that outlines the kind of care you'd like to get in the near future. To get started, you'll want to check in with your body so that you can connect with what it needs. Close your eyes and review your body from head to toe. Consider your head, neck, shoulders, arms, hands, torso, hips, legs, and feet—which areas are calling for attention? Do you need a haircut or color? How about an eye appointment? Is a massage in order? Has it been too long since you've had a physical exam or a Pap smear?

Once you have an idea of what needs to be done, make a list of the top-five items you'd like to handle over the next few months. If you're concerned about a particular issue, then the first item on your list needs to be calling a friend or family member for support. For example, when my client Leah decided to overcome her fear and get her first mammogram at the age of 51, she called her sister and asked her to hold her accountable for making the appointment. Then she had her sister go with her for emotional support.

Post your health plan in a place where you'll see it and, based on your schedule and finances, begin to book these appointments accordingly.

Resources

* WebMD (**www.webmd.com**)—a reliable resource that provides a variety of health and medical information.

* Women to Women (**www.womentowomen.com**)—a great Website devoted to women's health that combines alternative and traditional care to support mind, body, and spirit.

* Dr. Mehmet Oz's show on XM Satellite Radio—found on the Oprah & Friends Network, this terrific program offers a wide variety of emotional, physical, and spiritual health advice.

* ReachMD on XM Satellite Radio—an innovative communications company that provides thought-provoking medical news and information to health-care practitioners 24/7.

* The World Center for Emotional Freedom Techniques (**www.emofree.com**)—dedicated to the new "tapping therapies" (Emotional Freedom Techniques, or EFT) that can help with anything from insomnia and phobias to anxiety, panic attacks, and cravings.

* *EatingWell*—this magazine is filled with recipes, healthy cooking ideas, and weight-loss strategies to help you enjoy tasty yet nutritious meals.

* *The Mind-Body Makeover Project: A 12-Week Plan for Transforming Your Body and Your Life,* by Michael Gerrish—a comprehensive program for uncovering and conquering hidden obstacles to losing weight and getting fit.

* *YOU: Staying Young: The Owner's Manual for Extending Your Warranty,* by Michael F. Roizen, M.D., and Mehmet C. Oz, M.D.—one in a series dedicated to educating readers about their bodies and creating health and wellness.

* *Women's Bodies, Women's Wisdom: Creating Physical and Emotional Health and Healing,* by Christiane Northrup, M.D.—one of my all-time favorite health books for women.

Chapter Ten

Does That Anger Taste Good?

While shopping for clothes one quiet afternoon, I encountered a frustrated worker who decided to take her irritation out on me. As I left a dressing room with some items on my arm, the young woman yelled—actually yelled—at me for not putting them on a nearby return rack. When I started to explain that I was, in fact, buying the clothes, she abruptly interrupted me and continued her reprimand in a condescending tone: "I told you to put them right here!"

Immediately, I felt the signal in my body letting me know that I needed to speak up. I used to ignore the tightness in my neck and shoulders, but not anymore. Recognizing that this girl had crossed the line of appropriateness, I quickly said (in a very firm voice), "Stop and listen to me. I said that I plan to purchase these clothes. Please don't speak to me that way."

She looked up, surprised by my response, and replied, "Oh, sorry. No big deal." Then she proceeded to go about her business.

No big deal? I thought. *What's up with people today?* Yet I walked out of that dressing room feeling clear and empowered instead of blindsided and upset. Rather than do what I used to do—walk away with *her* frustration in my body—I left it where it belonged and continued my shopping.

Later that night when I shared the story with my friend Max, we talked about how so many people, especially women, put up with inappropriate behavior. Instead of speaking up (a reasonable response to rudeness), the desire to avoid conflict or to protect another's feelings takes precedence. So we keep our mouths shut and swallow our anger—a choice that has serious, long-term consequences. Friendships erode over time under the weight of unspoken hurt feelings, marriages dissolve from the disabling pain of chronic resentment, or health suffers as we make our way to the fridge one more time to shove down our anger with food.

Over the years I've learned to pay close attention to the messages I get from my body, so I know when to take care of myself by speaking up (and I also know when to practice restraint). I've come to recognize the warning signs that tell me what to do.

How about you? What are the common signals your body gives you when faced with inappropriate behavior? Do you get tightness in your throat, a rush of anxiety down your arms, or a flushed feeling in your face? As you raise your level of awareness, you'll find that your body becomes an ally, a barometer of sorts that tells you when and how unsolicited criticism, a snide remark, or a sharp reprimand may need to be addressed.

Freeze!

What's your typical reaction to sarcasm, insensitive comments, or inappropriate behavior? If you're like most people, you've probably found yourself in a situation where someone makes an unexpected rude comment and you suddenly freeze up. You stand there like a statue, completely immobilized and unable to say a word. When I talk to women about expressing their anger, this is the most common scenario they describe. They get blindsided by a bully, for example, are stunned into silence, and end up beating themselves up for not saying anything. Or they spend hours thinking about what they

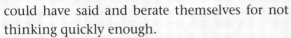

could have said and berate themselves for not thinking quickly enough.

When someone is rude, it's not uncommon to be rendered speechless. It's as if a part of our brain says, "Wait, he didn't just say *that,* did he?" or "I couldn't possibly have heard her right." It makes sense that we'd have a hard time quickly processing and reacting to a comment that goes so against our nature.

The all-too-familiar experience that triggers an old response could also be at work here. In other words, if you had a parent or caretaker who had a tendency toward sudden outbursts, sarcasm, or humiliating you in front of others, you may have learned *not* to react in order to stay safe. Silence may have been your best defense. As an adult, when someone portrays a similar behavior that triggers this past experience, you snap back into your old way of responding. Suddenly you're 8 years old instead of 40, and your way to cope is to keep your mouth shut.

Regardless of why you keep quiet, it's too expensive to swallow your anger. There are few things that will erode self-esteem more quickly than tolerating inappropriate behavior. Whether you say something right away or wait until later when you've had a chance to compose yourself or process your feelings, Extreme Self-Care means using your voice.

I've found that a simple approach works best, so the next time you're faced with rude behavior, try this:

1. Stop and acknowledge what just happened—don't stuff it. Before you say anything, give yourself a minute to take in what you've heard. If it feels right to do so, move on to the next step. Otherwise, take care of yourself by walking away without engaging the person at all so that you can find someone safe to talk to.

2. Take a deep breath and state what's on your mind (with grace and love whenever possible). Using the word *I,* say what you need to say. You might need to tell someone to stop his or her behavior with something like, "I can't believe you just spoke to me like that, and I need you to know it's not okay." Or you may need to stop someone from embarrassing you in public by saying, "I'm not willing to have this conversation with you here, and I'm asking you to stop so we can find a private spot."

3. Don't try to change the other person, get him or her to see your side, or defend your position. Stay on your end of the issue by simply expressing your feelings and what you need to have happen in order to feel respected and safe.

4. Walk away if necessary.

In the beginning, as you learn to speak up, you're bound to make mistakes. You may be too abrupt, you might stumble through the words, overexplain yourself, or say the wrong thing. Relax, you're human—this is just a normal part of the learning process. If you screw up, be big enough to apologize later on if you don't feel good about how you handled a situation. The important thing to remember is that *no one has the right to unload his or her frustration, stress, or "bad day" on you.* A simple response such as, "Please stop; that's not okay with me," is a fine way to start the process of protecting yourself.

The Power of Restraint

When you've been the recipient of rude behavior, the goal is to speak up rather than swallow your anger and end up causing harm to your body and soul. But what do you do when your buttons get pushed and you're tempted to fly off the handle and be rude yourself? How do you practice Extreme Self-Care when you want to strangle the person? The goal is to keep your self-respect intact.

Sometimes the circumstances warrant an immediate response. Yet there are other times—when you're caught off guard and you feel blindsided, or when you realize that your emotional reaction is exaggerated because an old wound has been triggered—when it's crucial to step back and get centered before you blow your top and end up regretting your behavior later on.

There are times in life when a good dose of restraint goes a long way in saving relationships, both with yourself and others. For example, I remember a conversation I had with a fellow coach who'd received an e-mail that made her angry. Fortunately, she had the good sense to call me before firing back a response. As we talked about the situation (a colleague had seemingly taken credit for her idea), I suggested that restraint might be a wise choice in handling the situation. Before she confronted this person with an accusation of betrayal, she needed to step back, regain her composure, and think clearly about how best to respond.

I'm sure that you've had similar experiences. Maybe a co-worker said something stupid to you in front of your peers, and you got so angry that you stormed out of the room. Or you found yourself in the middle of the same old argument with your son or daughter and heard yourself shouting foolish things that you knew you'd be sorry for later on. These are the times when restraint can be a valuable tool—one that saves energy and a whole lot of hurt feelings.

You'll know that restraint is a wise choice when:

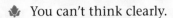

- You can't think clearly.

- You feel like screaming.

- Your emotional reaction feels bigger than what the current situation warrants.

- You feel anxiety coursing through your veins and you feel *compelled* to react.

- You feel angry and know there's a good chance you'll say something mean or stupid that you'll later regret.

We all get our buttons pushed. It's just a part of life. But the growth lies in our ability to make better choices.

Here are a few things you can do to ensure that you practice Extreme Self-Care by expressing your anger responsibly so that you can protect your relationship with yourself and others:

1. Close your eyes and breathe. When you're caught off guard, your body's fight-or-flight system gets activated, and it's as though all systems suddenly go on red alert. This means that you're operating in survivor mode—not conducive to making wise, thoughtful choices. By closing your eyes and taking several slow, deep breaths,

you'll immediately cause your brain to begin making alpha waves, the kind of patterns that gently calm you down.

2. Find a safe person to vent to about the situation. *Safe* is the operative word here. Be sure to choose someone who can listen well and allow you to process your feelings. Don't choose someone who simply fuels the drama by egging you on with his or her opinions of how you've been wronged.

3. Get more information. Before you confront the other person, ask questions. For example, if an e-mail pushed your buttons, ask the sender what he or she intended to communicate. By now most of us know that we miss the nuances and tone of a person's message when we communicate electronically. Make sure you have the facts before accusing someone of a damaging act. When my friend who was angry with her colleague for taking her idea calmed down and inquired about what happened, for instance, she discovered that her idea hadn't been taken at all. Her name had mistakenly been left out of a document.

4. Have a sane conversation with the person involved. Remember to speak from the "I" position and simply let him or her know how you feel and what you need. If the connection is important, also remember to start your exchange by acknowledging the value of the relationship first.

My sister, Kerri, has a sign in her office that says, LET IT GET COLD! It serves as a reminder to let the dust settle before she reacts. So the next time you find yourself in "overreaction mode," press the pause button. By choosing to step back and put some space between you and an immediate response, you not only protect your relationships, you preserve your self-respect, too.

Extreme Self-Care Challenge: Use Your Voice

This month is all about speaking your truth, and yes, it might mean expressing your anger as well. Now, I'm not suggesting that you go looking for a fight. The idea is to become more aware of those circumstances where you need to be a good steward for your Extreme Self-Care.

There are a variety of scenarios that may challenge you to speak up rather than swallow your anger. When I asked a group of friends for examples, here's what they had to say:

- "When someone cuts in line at a store."

- "When my boss asks me to do the work of three people without giving me more money or the resources I need to do the job well."

- "When a friend comments negatively on what I'm wearing."

- "When my teenager is disrespectful."

- "When my wife starts attacking my character rather than telling me what I need to do to support her."

- "When my employee doesn't follow through with a project that I've given him."

- "When my family members tease me about my marriage."

- "When a co-worker talks about me behind my back."

- "When my mother criticizes my parenting style."

Think about a recent example when you knew you needed to speak up but swallowed your anger instead. What do you wish you could have said? How would you handle the encounter differently now that you've learned a few new strategies?

This month, make a firm decision to no longer swallow your anger. Using the guidelines in this chapter, speak up and take a stand for your soul. Each time you do, write about the experience in your journal or notebook so that you can keep track of your success. Recording a list of accomplishments when it comes to expressing yourself fully and reviewing them on a regular basis is a great way to build self-esteem.

Resources

* *Growing Yourself Back Up: Understanding Emotional Regression,* by John Lee—a wonderful work about emotional regression and what you can do to respond instead of react when your buttons get pushed.

* *The Dance of Anger: A Woman's Guide to Changing the Patterns of Intimate Relationships,* by Harriet Lerner, Ph.D.—this classic is a must-read for both women and men.

* *Feel the Fear and Do It Anyway: Dynamic Techniques for Turning Fear, Indecision, and Anger into Power, Action, and Love* (8-CD set), by Susan Jeffers, Ph.D.—helps you become more powerful in the face of your fears.

* *Facing the Fire: Experiencing and Expressing Anger Appropriately,* by John Lee, with Bill Stott—shows you how anger can be expressed so safely and completely that it leads not to pain but to strength, increased energy, deeper communication with those we value, and personal serenity.

Chapter Eleven

Wake Up!

Many of us lose sight of the things that make us truly happy. Our interests and desires get put to sleep as we do our best to get through the stress of daily living. One of the great benefits of practicing Extreme Self-Care is that it starts to afford us the time, space, and energy to devote to the things we feel passionate about—those dreams or aspirations that may have been lost over the years. The challenge is knowing where to look for them when we finally come out from under our busy lives. Here's one way it happened for me.

As I was practicing better self-care during my husband's illness, I uncovered one of my passions in an unexpected place: a department store. A week before Christmas, we were shopping for a few last-minute decorations. While walking through the women's department, I came across a beautifully made black-and-white tweed hat, which sported a wide pleated band above the brim, finished with a big plaid bow. I've always been drawn to hats, especially classic designs, and this one was unusually smart. I immediately tried it on, and it fit perfectly. I fell in love with this hat until I looked at the price—it was far more expensive than seemed reasonable. So I put it back, and Michael and I finished our shopping.

As the holidays rolled around, every now and then I'd think about the hat. I'd remember its design, the feel of its fabric, and the way it fit on my head. I kept thinking, *Why is this hat so important?* Then I'd let it go.

Right after the new year, I woke up thinking about the hat again. Since I had the morning to myself, I decided to go back to the department store to see if I could find it on sale. I figured that if it had stayed with me this long, I at least owed it to myself to have another look. So off I went.

When I arrived at the store, I browsed around a bit but could see that the hat was gone. Being a persistent woman when I get an idea in my mind, however, I went to speak with a clerk about it. She remembered that the dress hats had been moved to a new part of the store. *Great!* I thought. *Maybe it's there.* I raced to her suggested section, but the hat was nowhere to be found.

In a last-ditch effort to appease my inner longing, I asked another employee if she'd seen any dress hats. She looked at me with big brown eyes, smiled, and moving her hands about her head, asked, "Big hat or small hat?" Realizing that she didn't speak English that well, I attempted to describe the hat as best I could. She waved for me to follow her to a storage room in the rear of the building. As I eagerly waited outside, hoping for good news, I heard her repeat, "Big hat, big hat, big hat," over and over again to someone in the back. Suddenly the door burst open, and there stood this sweet woman with a carriage full of dress hats. Perched prominently on top of the pile? My black-and-white hat!

I took the hat as if it were made of glass, thanked the woman, and headed for the front of the store. Looking at the price tag, I was happy to discover that the hat was now 30 percent off. Content, I paid for it and headed to my car.

I placed my purchase on the passenger seat next to me and stared at it for several minutes. While the hat was beautiful, it wasn't spectacular, and I wondered what in the world was so darn compelling about it. That's when it hit me: this hat was trying to tell me something. So I asked it. Yes, as strange as it sounds, I looked over at it and said out loud, "Hey hat, what are you trying to tell me?"

As I waited for an answer, tears filled my eyes. A memory flashed in my mind of being 18 years old and arriving at work in a purple dress with a matching hat and coat. It was a time in my life when I loved clothes and putting outfits together with the right accessories. As I revisited that time, I realized something important: my quest wasn't about this hat; it was about reawakening a part of myself I'd put to sleep long ago. The hat was just a symbol—a clue pointing me to where I needed to look. It was about resurrecting my love of color and art in the form of apparel. It was about honoring the part of me who loves to watch fashion and design shows over and over again, who cuts out images of classic outfits from magazines when making a treasure map, and who loves to fantasize about creating beautiful clothes.

Now, was I going to stop writing books and become a fashion designer? Unlikely. But that wasn't the point. The whole experience—from first seeing that hat to thinking about it all the time, going to unusual lengths to find it in the store, and finally taking the time to figure out what it represented—compelled me to do something important: give a hidden part of me permission to wake up and be heard!

❦

What parts of you may be lurking beneath the surface? Start with what you love to see, hear, touch, taste, or smell. Maybe your love of essential oils is trying to lead you down the path of making your own custom blends. Whether you sell them or not doesn't matter—it's the interest and the desire that needs to be honored. Or maybe the passion that drove you to become a vegan is calling upon you to take the next step and begin teaching classes about this new lifestyle choice.

Now, expressing that part of you doesn't mean you have to stop everything and dedicate your life to this one cause. Perhaps you just need to give yourself permission to redecorate a room so that you can play around with your love of interior design, or to volunteer at a local rescue shelter so that you can spend time in an environment that feeds your love of animals.

When I originally shared my hat adventure with my online community, I was struck by the response. Not only did I receive lots of mail, but the feedback let me know that I'd clearly touched a nerve. Men wrote about their own love of fashion and the frustration they experienced in not being comfortable with expressing it. Women shared the deep sadness they felt at letting their busy lives short-circuit their dreams.

One community member told me she realized that a doll she kept on the bureau in her bedroom was a link to a hidden love of sewing that she'd given up long ago. Another gentleman admitted that his passion for *American Idol* reflected his love of songwriting; recognizing this, he started making music again instead of listening to the critical inner voice that said he was too old at 52.

My black-and-white hat was symbolic of a hidden love of fashion and design. What might be a clue for you? Now that you've dedicated so much of yourself to practicing better self-care, it shouldn't be too difficult to find an image, a symbol, or a repetitive experience that's attempting to get your attention. Then once you uncover a passion worth pursuing, you'll be ready to take action so that you can breathe life into your desire. It's time to wake up!

Extreme Self-Care Challenge: Discover a Hidden Passion

So how about it? Are you ready to see what dreams or desires are waiting to be uncovered, rediscovered, or reawakened in you? This month I want you to do two things:

—First, I want you to **go on a little treasure hunt.** Keep your eyes open for a symbol or object that reflects an inner part of you that longs to be expressed. Notice when something catches your eye in a window, when an image online or on TV causes you to look again, or when a photo in a magazine or catalog pulls at your heart. Maybe there's an item you keep around the house that's so close you don't even realize it, or the clue might be hidden out of sight. Go through your closets, boxes in the basement, or drawers you haven't looked in for a while.

Once you have an image or symbol, bring it into your life. If you don't have a photo of the item or idea, go online and search for one. Ask yourself, "If this image or object could speak, what would it tell me?" Write down whatever occurs to you.

—Once you've uncovered a part of you that's ready to be resurrected, **do something to wake it up.** As soon as I understood what the black-and-white hat was trying to tell me, for example, I knew I had to fuel my passion. So here's what I did:

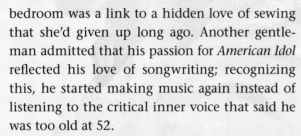 I called my cousin Karen, a gifted seamstress, and asked her to help me work on a simple project—a duvet cover for my bed—so that I could begin to understand the basics of sewing. We set up a time to visit a fabric store in order for me to learn about different materials, fabrics, tools, and supplies.

🌿 Jay Calderin, who is a member of my online community as well as an accomplished fashion designer and teacher at the School of Fashion Design in Boston, invited me to have tea with him to talk about ways to awaken my "inner fashionista." I took him up on the offer and enjoyed a tour of the design center and great conversation.

🌿 I spent an afternoon going through several fashion magazines and cutting out the images that I loved the most.

🌿 I created a treasure map filled with these favorite images, along with inspiring slogans to motivate me to keep pursuing this passion.

Using my list above as inspiration, identify three things you could do this month to pursue your desire further. If your image is a baseball, it might be time to investigate adult baseball leagues. If you seem to always be on the lookout for great pens and paper, there may be a writer in you who needs to come out. If you're not sure what to do, brainstorm with friends or members of your Life Makeover Group for ideas. You can also go online and find message boards or community lists of people who share your interest.

There's a good chance that you'll be pleasantly surprised by the doors that open to support your commitment to reawaken this hidden part of you. It's all about where you put your focused intention. Once I decided to let my love of fashion see the light of day, all kinds of opportunities began to emerge. They will for you, too. When you take steps to honor your soul, the Universe will be right behind you!

Resources

🌿 *Finding Your Passion*—my award-winning audio program outlines a practical plan to uncover and express your passion.

🌿 *The Gifted Adult: A Revolutionary Guide for Liberating Everyday Genius,* by Mary-Elaine Jacobsen, Psy.D.—shows gifted adults how to identify and free their extraordinary potential.

❀ *The Alchemist,* by Paulo Coelho—a wonderful fable about staying true to your dreams.

❀ *Three Cups of Tea: One Man's Mission to Promote Peace . . . One School at a Time,* by Greg Mortenson and David Oliver Relin—a must-read for everyone. This book demonstrates the power of using passion to make a profound difference in the world.

❀ TED (**www.ted.com**)—one of my favorite Websites, where the world's greatest thinkers and doers gather for inspiration.

Chapter Twelve

Your Extreme Self-Care First-Aid Kit

N ow that you've become better equipped at practicing the art of Extreme Self-Care, there's something important you should know before we finish our work together: when life hands you a challenge, a crisis, or an unexpected curveball, there's a good chance you'll forget everything you've learned from this book.

People you love will die. Jobs may be lost. Geographical moves might be forced upon you by a partner's career change. An unexpected medical diagnosis may throw your world into a tailspin. That's just the way life works here on planet Earth. These are the times when we need the practice of Extreme Self-Care the most—when we're feeling scared, unsteady, and desperate to find a way back to center. That's when we need an Extreme Self-Care First-Aid Kit.

While working on this final chapter, I had a chance to use my own kit. During a routine mammogram, my doctor discovered a lump in my right breast and recommended that I undergo a biopsy to rule out cancer. This news was unexpected and frightening, and the hardest part of all was waiting three days to get the results of the test. During the wait, I felt so out of control and afraid. At night I fought to manage my worried mind as I lay in the dark trying to sleep. And in the mornings I woke up feeling anxious, nauseated, and ungrounded—as if floating in space, disconnected from my core.

The practice of Extreme Self-Care turned out to be my lifeline, steps that not only got me through the waiting period, but also better prepared me for whatever might happen. At the end of three days, I was fortunate enough to receive a clean bill of health, and the ordeal gave me the gift of knowing exactly what I needed to do to take good care of myself in a time of crisis. I'd like to help you discover what you need, too.

When you're most afraid, it's time to be kind and gentle with yourself. You've got to find a way to hold yourself in a safe and constructive manner while you handle the turmoil and strain. Extreme Self-Care during times of great stress means engaging in those activities that allow you to honor your feelings, the ones that connect you to your center and reattach you to something solid and secure.

An Extreme Self-Care First-Aid Kit is a well-prepared plan of action put in place *before* you need to use it. It consists of things you can do on a physical, emotional, and spiritual level that will give you comfort, connection, and a feeling of steadiness while navigating the rough waters of a crisis. When faced with a difficult period, what matters most is that you return to the behaviors and practices that reflect Extreme Self-Care as quickly as possible, so you can restore yourself to sanity and strength. That way, you'll bring your best, most resourceful self to the challenge at hand.

Creating Your Extreme Self-Care Kit

The Extreme Self-Care First-Aid Kit consists of ten ways to take good care of yourself when you need the most support. To create your kit, ask yourself the following questions:

1. Who can I turn to for support when I'm afraid? Who comforts me, makes me feel safe, and allows me to have my feelings?

2. Who do I need to avoid? Who adds to my anxiety level, overwhelms me with questions, or has a tough time just listening without interrupting or offering advice?

3. What does my body need to feel nurtured, strong, and healthy?

4. What responsibilities or commitments do I need to let go of to clear some space so that I'm able to feel my feelings and do what's necessary to honor my needs?

5. What unhelpful coping strategies or activities do I need to avoid?

6. What spiritual practice restores my faith or connects me with God or a Higher Power of my own understanding?

7. What do I need to feel comforted at this time?

8. How will I best express my feelings?

9. What object can I use as a talisman that will remind me to breathe, relax my thinking mind, and return my awareness to the present moment?

10. What can I do when I need to take a break from the emotional stress? What's my best healthy distraction?

The answers to these questions will help you formulate a plan of action that you can use when faced with a big life challenge.

∞

Let's look at three different examples of an Extreme Self-Care First-Aid Kit. The first is from Sarah. Here's how she answered the questions:

1. *I need to call my best friend, Sandy, and let her know what's going on when I feel overwhelmed or afraid.*

2. *I need to avoid talking about the situation with my co-workers, who get caught up in the drama of my problems.*

3. *I need to remember to drink lots of water and take my vitamins, something I forget to do when I feel overwhelmed. I also want to go to yoga at least twice a week to stay centered.*

4. *I need to arrange to have my neighbors help out with driving the kids to and from school, and I have to say no to any new request of my time for at least a month.*

5. *I need to stop watching TV late at night so I get enough sleep.*

6. *I need to listen to the inspirational playlists I've created on my iPod.*

7. *I need to schedule a massage to help me relax and feel nurtured.*

8. *I'll use my journal to write down how I feel about what's going on.*

9. *I'll carry my favorite stone that I found on a beach years ago. It's in the shape of a heart, and it always makes me feel like someone's watching over me.*

10. *To distract myself from the stress, I need to take regular breaks to play with my dog, Winston.*

Next up is Paula. Paula not only wrote out her list, she also created three laminated cards with the following information. She put one in her journal, gave one to her best friend, and put one in the kitchen with other emergency information. Here's her Extreme Self-Care plan:

1. *My sister, Margaret, is my best option for support.*

2. *I need to avoid talking to my mom, who gets anxious when I'm upset.*

3. *I need to eat well, so I'll plan to get precooked food from my health-food store.*

4. *I'll look over my appointment book and eliminate anything that doesn't feel like an absolute yes.*

5. *I need to make sure that I don't overdo it by eating too much sugar.*

6. *I want to meditate for at least 20 minutes a day.*

7. *I need to give myself permission to work in my comfy clothes.*

8. *I need to talk about how I feel with safe people—I'll be sure to check in with my sister on a daily basis.*

9. *I'll keep my mala [prayer beads] with me for those times when I want to calm my worried mind.*

10. *My best healthy distraction is watching favorite movies from Netflix.*

Finally, Heidi took the idea of an Extreme Self-Care First-Aid Kit to a whole new level. After making her list, she found photographs that gave her a visual representation of each item, and then she created a digital page on her computer to use as a desktop display when she was in trouble. She also printed the collage out to keep with her. Here are her examples:

1. *I'll stay in touch with my mom—she's a good friend.*

2. *I need to set boundaries with my room-mate to keep her out of my business.*

3. *I'll stay connected to nature and be sure that I get enough sunlight by going for a run or walk in the state park near my home every chance I get.*

4. *I need to stop taking on any extra projects at work.*

5. *I need to limit the amount of caffeine I drink so that I don't add to my anxiety.*

6. *I want to get to more 12-step meetings during the week.*

7. *I'll take naps in the sun with my cat, Roxy, and use my electric blanket to warm my bed at night.*

8. *I'll talk more about how I'm feeling at my 12-step meetings.*

9. *My talisman is the picture of my deceased dad that I keep in a locket. I'll wear this around my neck to feel him with me.*

10. *I'll take a break from the stress by making beaded jewelry—something I love to do.*

As you can see, everyone has a different way of taking good care of themselves when under pressure. Let's see what you'll do. . . .

Extreme Self-Care Challenge: Create Your Own Kit

Now it's time to create your own Extreme Self-Care First-Aid Kit. Using the questions on page 103, formulate a list of ten things you can do to take extremely good care of yourself when going through a tough time. Then think about where you'll keep this list so that you can easily find it when you need it. You might even take Paula's advice and give a copy to your top support person—that way, you'll have someone else who can step in and help implement the plan should you be incapable of doing so yourself. Also, keep this list in a file on your computer and schedule an alert in your calendar at least every six months to remind you to review and update the list. And finally, trust me when I say that Extreme Self-Care is the perfect prescription for handling any life challenge.

Resources

* *On Grief and Grieving: Finding the Meaning of Grief Through the Five Stages of Loss,* by Elisabeth Kübler-Ross and David Kessler—an excellent resource to support the grief process.

* Al-Anon/Alateen (**www.al-anon.alateen.org**)—a great organization for those dealing with the addiction of a loved one.

* Alcoholics Anonymous (**www.aa.org**)—for those seeking support to stop drinking.

* Befrienders (**www.befrienders.org**)—a Website dedicated to providing help for those who are considering suicide and/or grappling with other life-threatening issues.

* The therapy directory on *Psychology Today* magazine's Website (**therapists.psychology today.com**)—for when you need to talk to a qualified professional.

Acknowledgments

It is with great pleasure and deep gratitude that I acknowledge the people who make a difference in my life and, therefore, in the lives of those who come in contact with my work.

I'd first like to thank Wanda Stevens for keeping me sane during two of the most difficult years of my life. Your love and support have made an enormous difference to me and my family, and your wisdom can be found throughout these pages. I'd also like to thank Kerri Richardson, a wise-beyond-her-years coach, for your love, unwavering support, creative collaboration, and friendship. I'm blessed to have a sister like you.

My personal editor, Marilyn Abraham, continues to be the best midwife a writer could have. I love you, M. Thanks also to Fran Massey, for "saving me from myself." I appreciate your feedback immensely. And finally, thank you to Shannon Littrell, my talented Hay House editor, for your professionalism, keen eye, and sensitivity to my words.

I am very lucky to have good people around me who take care of me and my company. Chris Barnes, a dear friend, is my trusted virtual assistant. Thank you for your integrity and caring heart, and for the wonderful way you support our community. Thank you to Holly Catalina, our e-commerce coordinator, for minding our online store. Your kindness and sensitivity are your greatest gifts. Thank you to Kelly O'Brien and Terry Nolan for keeping our Website up and running so smoothly. Robin Gillette is my financial maven, and one of the kindest people I know. You make such a difference in my life, and I thank you.

Many thanks to my literary team: Amanda Urban, the best agent in the world; and all the folks at ICM. Big gratitude goes to the wonderful people at Hay House: Louise Hay, Reid Tracy, Christy Salinas, Jill Kramer, Melissa Brinkerhoff, and everyone else who makes Hay House a joy to work with. I'd especially like to acknowledge my dear friend and Hay House Events Director, Nancy Levin. You are uniquely gifted at caring for others, and I love you, Nanny. And finally, thanks to my fun and fabulous radio crew: Summer McStravick, Diane Ray, Sonny Salinas, Steve Morris, Kyle Thompson, Joe Bartlett, Emily Manning, and Mitch Wilson.

My deepest gratitude goes to my friend and lawyer, Mark Lawless, who's always there to hold the lines when I let go. Thanks for the laughs and great advice. And thank you to Barry Coscia, for your financial counsel and sensitivity.

Thanks to Ania O'Connor and Annie Twiss for taking care of my body as I write, and to Deb LaChance for keeping the home fires burning. And a heartfelt thank you to Tim Ford, Mark Hovey, and Jake Long, who were there until the very end to help make our dream home (and my new writing retreat) a reality. I bless you every single day.

Thank you to my dear friends Nanna Aida Svendson, Pat Adler, Helen Gitkind, Ro Gordon, Kelly O'Brien, Connie Kelley, and Deirdre DiDonna—I don't know where I'd be without your unconditional love and support. Thank you to my parents, John and Ann Richardson, who have given me more gifts than you'll ever realize—gifts that are woven throughout the pages of this book. And to my loving in-laws, Curt and Pat Gerrish, I am blessed beyond measure to have you both in my life.

It's one thing to write a book that you hope will change lives for the better, and another to reach people in the far corners of the world. I remain deeply grateful to Oprah Winfrey for providing a vehicle to share my message.

My respect and gratitude goes to the members of my online community who have been so supportive over the years. Thank you for your e-mails and prayers, your valuable input and feedback, and for the heartfelt stories of how you're facing challenges in your own lives. I learn so much from each one of you, and I am inspired by your commitment to consciousness.

Bruce Kohl, Bob and Melissa Olson, and Melissa Silk have held my heart when I needed it most (and provided me with much-needed laughter, too!). Thank you for your treasured friendship. And to my best friend, Max Dilley, who demands that I show up fully in the world, I can't imagine my life without you, BH.

My cat, Poupon, has opened my heart in ways I never would have imagined. His beautiful energy is contained in these pages. Thank you, my angel disguised as a cat.

Michael, my husband, my love—as challenging as these past two years have been, I wouldn't trade the journey with you for anything in the world. Thank you for your love; your friendship; your editorial guidance; and, most of all, your deep commitment to the evolution of your soul. You are, and always will be, my everything.

And finally, and most important, I thank God—the Divine Force that continues to guide my life.

About the Author

Cheryl Richardson is the *New York Times* best-selling author of *Take Time for Your Life, Life Makeovers, Stand Up for Your Life,* and *The Unmistakable Touch of Grace.* She leads a large Web community at **www.cherylrichardson.com**, which is dedicated to helping people around the world improve their quality of life.

Notes

Notes

Notes

Hay House Titles of Related Interest

YOU CAN HEAL YOUR LIFE, the movie, starring Louise L. Hay & Friends
(available as a 1-DVD program and an expanded 2-DVD set)
Watch the trailer at: **www.LouiseHayMovie.com**

∞

THE AGE OF MIRACLES: Embracing the New Midlife, by Marianne Williamson

THE ASTONISHING POWER OF EMOTIONS: Let Your Feelings Be Your Guide,
by Esther and Jerry Hicks (The Teachings of Abraham®)

**CHANGE YOUR THOUGHTS—CHANGE YOUR LIFE:
Living the Wisdom of the Tao,** by Dr. Wayne W. Dyer

**FOUR ACTS OF PERSONAL POWER: How to Heal Your Past
and Create a Positive Future,** by Denise Linn

THE SECRET PLEASURES OF MENOPAUSE, by Christiane Northrup, M.D.

∞

All of the above are available at your local bookstore,
or may be ordered by contacting Hay House (see next page).

∞

We hope you enjoyed this Hay House book. If you'd like to receive a free catalog featuring additional Hay House books and products, or if you'd like information about the Hay Foundation, please contact:

Hay House, Inc.
P.O. Box 5100
Carlsbad, CA 92018-5100

(760) 431-7695 or **(800) 654-5126**
(760) 431-6948 (fax) or **(800) 650-5115 (fax)**
www.hayhouse.com® • **www.hayfoundation.org**

Published and distributed in Australia by: Hay House Australia Pty. Ltd., 18/36 Ralph St., Alexandria NSW 2015 • *Phone:* 612-9669-4299 • *Fax:* 612-9669-4144 • www.hayhouse.com.au

Published and distributed in the United Kingdom by: Hay House UK, Ltd., 292B Kensal Rd., London W10 5BE • *Phone:* 44-20-8962-1230 • *Fax:* 44-20-8962-1239 • www.hayhouse.co.uk

Published and distributed in the Republic of South Africa by: Hay House SA (Pty), Ltd., P.O. Box 990, Witkoppen 2068 • *Phone/Fax:* 27-11-467-8904 • orders@psdprom.co.za • www.hayhouse.co.za

Published in India by: Hay House Publishers India, Muskaan Complex, Plot No. 3, B-2, Vasant Kunj, New Delhi 110 070 • *Phone:* 91-11-4176-1620 • *Fax:* 91-11-4176-1630 • www.hayhouse.co.in

Distributed in Canada by: Raincoast, 9050 Shaughnessy St., Vancouver, B.C. V6P 6E5
Phone: (604) 323-7100 • *Fax:* (604) 323-2600 • www.raincoast.com

Tune in to **HayHouseRadio.com**® for the best in inspirational talk radio featuring top Hay House authors! And, sign up via the Hay House USA Website to receive the Hay House online newsletter and stay informed about what's going on with your favorite authors. You'll receive bimonthly announcements about Discounts and Offers, Special Events, Product Highlights, Free Excerpts, Giveaways, and more!
www.hayhouse.com®

To:

HAY HOUSE, INC.
P.O. Box 5100
Carlsbad, CA 92018-5100

HAY
HOUSE